How I Became an American Socialist

Garry Leech

Published by Misfit Books
South Bar, Nova Scotia, Canada
Copyright © 2016 Garry Leech
All rights reserved.
ISBN-13: 978-0995000100

For my children and grandchildren
Johan, Owen, Morgan, Kathleen and Dylan

CONTENTS

	Acknowledgments	vii
	Introduction	1
1	The Early Years	4
2	The Few, the Proud, and the Ugly	16
3	My Salvadoran Nightmare	26
4	Tying and Untying the Knot	41
5	Welcome to the Jungle	51
6	My Political Awakening	61
7	From Gandhi to Che	83
8	Death at Home and Abroad	94
9	The Day that Shook the World	105
10	The Home Front	120
11	The Capitalist Genocide	126
12	From Fatherhood to Socialism	143
13	An American in Havana	158
	Conclusion: A Few Final Thoughts …	176
	About the Author	191
	Index	192

ACKNOWLEDGMENTS

My life journey has been a long and winding road that has been influenced by far too many people to mention here. Nevertheless, there are some who merit special thanks. First and foremost among those who have significantly influenced the person I have become are my parents Gerald and Norma and my brother Don and sister Karyn. I also owe a great debt to my longtime friend Stephen Paul for many years of positive influence and for always challenging me on every level. The most sincerest gratitude must go to my loving partner Terry Gibbs for her constant inspiration and ceaseless support for both me as a person and for my work. Similarly, I would not be the person I am today without my beautiful children Johan, Owen and Morgan and grandchildren Kathleen and Dylan. I also owe a special thanks to my good friends Stephen Law and Evelyn Jones for their constant inspiration and support. Finally, many thanks to all the other friends who have influenced me significantly on my journey through this wonderful adventure called life.

"At the risk of seeming ridiculous, let me say that the true revolutionary is guided by a great feeling of love. It is impossible to think of a genuine revolutionary lacking this quality."

—Ernesto "Che" Guevara

INTRODUCTION

I AM A SOCIALIST! There, I said it. It's not something that people in North America tend to profess, even if they are prone to such political leanings. Socialism is an ideological system that is somewhat more palatable in Europe as well as in parts of Latin America, Africa and Asia. But in North America, and in the United States in particular, confessing to being a socialist in most circles is akin to admitting that one has leprosy. But at the time of this writing I am not in North America, I am in Havana.

I am spending the summer of 2015 in Havana. It seems like a logical place for a socialist to be. But before I can explain how this American socialist ended up living temporarily in a small two-bedroom apartment in Cuba's capital there is an important question that must be asked: What is socialism? Is it an ideology that advocates authoritarian political systems that impose conformity in thought and action upon the population at large? Or is socialism a democratic system that seeks to ensure that everyone has a meaningful voice in all of the major decisions that impact their lives and that everyone's basic needs are fulfilled in an ecologically sustainable manner? Sure, there have been some failed socialist experiments that reflected the traits of the former definition, the Soviet

Union being one of them. But capitalist societies, including the United States, have also been dominated by such characteristics. For me though, it is the latter definition that represents a more accurate description of socialism. But this book does not seek to provide a precise definition of socialism, rather it seeks to explain why someone living in North America might become a socialist in the 21st century. At least it attempts to explain how that transformation occurred for this particular socialist. In short, it's the story of the experiences in my life that led to my political awakening and the eventual realization of the fact that I am a socialist.

Like many others in North America and Western Europe who grew up against the backdrop of the Cold War, I viewed socialists, or "communists," as evil authoritarian warmongers who were out to destroy the freedom-loving peoples of the world. After all, the Soviet Union was, as President Ronald Reagan famously stated, the "evil empire." Consequently, as a result of my upbringing in Britain and the United States, I internalized many of the values that were promulgated by the governments, education systems and media in these capitalist nations. It wasn't until many years later, and after numerous transformative experiences in Latin America, that I came to seriously question the dominant narrative of these capitalist societies and to begin dissecting the hypocrisies, contradictions and outright lies.

Becoming a father only increased my concerns about the state of the world and what the future holds in store for all of us. Growing global inequality and other social injustices, along with the emerging threat of climate change, led me to envision a more democratic, humane and sustainable alternative for the sake of my children and

INTRODUCTION

grandchildren. I am not alone with such concerns about the destructiveness of capitalism and its consequences for our future. The emergence of the Occupy and the indigenous-led Idle No More movements in North America attest to this reality. As do the mass protests by the *indignados* against the austerity measures imposed on Spain and Greece. This concern is also evident in the US presidential candidacy of self-proclaimed socialist Bernie Sanders and the election of socialist Jeremy Corbyn as leader of Britain's Labour Party.

Further evidence of the dissatisfaction with capitalism and desire for an alternative was presented in a 2011 Pew Research Center Poll, which revealed that more young Americans (18-29 year olds) preferred socialism than capitalism. While 49 percent viewed socialism positively, only 46 percent viewed capitalism the same way. The reasons for the growing support for socialism among youth in the United States most likely rests in the discrediting of capitalism that resulted from the economic crisis of 2008 and the fact that young Americans' perception of socialism is not tainted by the failed Soviet experiment.

But before I begin defining in depth what socialism in the 21st century means to me, I first need to provide the historical context that led me to reach such a radical conclusion. In other words, I need to explain how my political awakening came about. And to do that, I need to begin at the beginning.

CHAPTER 1

The Early Years

Obviously, I was not born a socialist. But I was born white. And I was born a male. I was also born into the middle class. These realities, as much as anything, have marked my life. This set of circumstances came into being when I was born in Coventry, England on April 26, 1960. I arrived on this earth at 8:52 p.m. precisely. Of this my mother is certain because the clock on the wall of the delivery room stopped at the exact moment of my birth. I'm not sure of the significance of such an ominous omen, but I'm pretty certain the thought that their newborn son would grow up to become a socialist never entered the minds of my parents.

My parents were both born and raised in the industrial city of Coventry during the Great Depression and World War Two. I grew up listening to tales of war-time rationing and bombing raids by the German Luftwaffe. They grew up in British working-class households and, having come of age following the war, benefitted greatly from Keynesian policies that established the so-called welfare state and bountiful opportunities with regards to education, apprenticeships and jobs. Not surprisingly, they responded in the same manner as many others who grew up during those difficult times: they took advantage of government programs and incentives as well as the post-war economic boom to ensure that they would never again endure economic hardship. And, also like so many others of their generation, they quickly attained middle-class status, and so we lived the life of a typical suburban family.

Less than one year after my arrival in this world my brother Don was born. I don't know if it was the shock of having us boys so close together, but it was another six years before our sister Karyn arrived on the scene. Don and I spent the early years of our childhood in the Coventry area where our father Gerald worked as an engineer for the multinational tractor manufacturer Massey Ferguson. Our mother Norma, when she wasn't a stay-at-home mum, would perform secretarial work for a legal firm. One year after Karyn was born we made our first major move away from the place of our births and away from our relatively large extended family.

I was eight-years-old when we moved north to a suburb of Manchester called Bramhall. I was a bonafide soccer fanatic and the move took me to the city of my favorite soccer team Manchester United which, that same year, became the first English team to win the European Cup. But the depressing decline in my favorite team's performance during the ensuing years was offset by my growing interest in girls and music.

By the time I was twelve my sexual curiosity had led me to become more conscious of females my own age; and of those one or two grades ahead of me in school. For me and my male friends, our female counterparts had evolved from yucky, boring, incomprehensible creatures that were to be avoided at all costs into sexy, attractive, incomprehensible ravens to drool over. In other words, those girls were nothing more than objects of our obsessive adolescent sexual desires. And while I clearly understood why my friends and I were utterly obsessed with girls, I certainly couldn't see any reason to be envious of the other sex. After all, who would want to be subjected daily to gawking eyes, lewd comments and overt sexual harassment by a bunch of drooling adolescent boys with pock-marked faces?

During those years glam rock performers like David Bowie, T. Rex, Roxy Music, Mott the Hoople, Cockney Rebel and Slade were at their zenith. Being a typically trendy British lad, I routinely dressed in the requisite baggy pants and high-heeled platform shoes that represented the uniform of glam rockers and rebellious teens at the time. Like most teens obsessed with music and fashion I was convinced that I was a rebel of some sort or another and that my defiance toward my parents' generation, and society in general, was most strongly symbolized by the music I chose to listen to and the clothes that I wore.

I was also a product of the British education system, which largely portrayed the unearned white middle-class male privilege bestowed on me at birth as my natural right. My history and social studies classes also imbibed in me the belief that Britain was the greatest nation in the world because it had ruled the waves and a third of the planet's land mass. My teachers failed to fully convey the degree to which Britain's mighty empire had crumbled by the time I entered school. However, this reality would later become evident to me; and apparently to my grandfather too. Upon entering the Dominican Republic in the 1980s for a vacation with my mother and father, who had recently become Canadian citizens, the immigration agent told my parents that they could stay in the country for up to six months because they were Canadians, but my grandfather's British passport only permitted him to remain for three months. Apparently, my grandfather responded indignantly to this affront to his imperial pride by declaring, "There was a time when the British could go anywhere!"

My grandfather was also white and male, but distinctly working class. He worked for forty years in the factories of industrial Coventry and was an ardent supporter of unions and the old Labour Party. But like many working class Brits he exhibited contradictory attitudes towards the capitalist system under which he toiled, particularly throughout the Great Depression and World War Two. On the one hand he was a harsh critic of the exploitation of workers by the capitalist "bosses," while on the other hand he was an ardent flag-waving patriot who believed in the superiority of Britain and its empire. Even a working-class white male in Britain possesses a greater degree of privilege than the overwhelming majority of the world's population. This reality is evident in the many opportunities that white working-class British males have traditionally enjoyed when emigrating to former colonies such as the United States, Canada, Australia and New Zealand; opportunities that are often not available to indigenous peoples and other non-whites born in those nations.

In 1975, when I was fifteen, my family followed the path of so many others before them by making the move to the "New World" to further improve our lot in life. I had mixed feelings about the move. I'd met my first true love, Shona, six months earlier and was distraught at the thought of leaving her and my friends. However, I despised the English school system and, as a result, was barely a "C" student. My attitude toward school left my parents dreading parent-teacher conferences. Every year they would be forced to listen to my teachers dutifully inform them that "Garry has the ability, but simply won't apply himself." Consequently, with only six months remaining before I had to sit my "O" Level examinations, and faced with the very real and embarrassing prospect of failing many of them, the idea of fleeing across the Atlantic Ocean took on a certain appeal. And so we packed up our belongings and made what at that time was still considered to be a relatively major move for a family.

We left the middle-class suburbs of industrial Manchester and settled into the middle-class suburbs of industrial Detroit courtesy of my father's job with Massey Ferguson. We bought a bigger house and bigger cars and very quickly came to epitomize the individualistic atomized suburban American family. My father's engineering career was progressing nicely and he was being rewarded both financially and with greater responsibilities in management. And while there were cultural challenges in our move to the Midwestern United States, for the most part we continued life as upstanding members of the white middle class.

For me, the move to Detroit created a greater awareness of non-whites and, as a consequence, of my own whiteness. I first became conscious of overt racism immediately after arriving in the United States. One of the appealing aspects of crossing the Atlantic Ocean had been the thought of living in Motown. In addition to British rock music, I also loved Black American music including the Motown sound of Stevie Wonder, Marvin Gaye, Smokey Robinson, the Temptations and others. But it wasn't Detroit itself that I moved to; rather it was a suburb twenty miles outside the city center called Northville. I was woefully ignorant about the United States. What little awareness I possessed had been mostly garnered from Hollywood movies and TV shows. Therefore, I was ill-prepared for the social and cultural reality of both Detroit, the state of Michigan and the US Midwest in general.

Northville High School was overwhelmingly white. In fact, I don't think a single black person lived in the suburb of twelve thousand people. I quickly realized that most of Detroit's other suburbs were just as white. Essentially, there was an invisible barrier that encircled Detroit's city limits behind which was contained the Black population. There were very few whites living in the city of Detroit and virtually no Blacks in its lilywhite suburbs. There existed an unofficial, yet very real, apartheid structure.

During the civil rights struggles of the 1960s, riots had erupted in numerous US cities. The explosion against institutional and culturally-based racism occurred in Detroit in 1967 and led to the deployment of the National Guard to inner city neighborhoods. The conflict resulted in the deaths of forty-three people, while almost twelve hundred were injured. Many whites responded by abandoning the city and moving to the surrounding suburbs. Thereafter, Detroit became a Black city and the entire metropolitan area was marked by racial tension. Urban Blacks despised the racist structures and attitudes that persevered despite the civil rights movement's legal gains, and suburban whites both feared and resented "uppity" Blacks who no longer passively accepted their "place" in US society. It was into this racial cauldron that our family moved in 1975.

I arrived for my first day at Northville High School attired in high-heeled platform shoes, black baggy pants, a dress shirt with long pointed collars and a blazer. These were the fashionable clothes worn by many white teenage males in Britain at the time, but when I walked into my new school I immediately felt as though I'd been beamed Star Trek-like onto the surface of another planet. While there was no official school uniform policy, there was an unofficial dress code that virtually all of my fellow students strictly adhered to: Tee-shirt, blue jeans and sneakers. I quickly learned that in the eyes of my peers I was dressed as only a black pimp in Detroit would dress. The only thing I was lacking, they happily informed me, was the fedora and a pink Cadillac.

The racism exhibited by my fellow students was not limited to fashion, it also applied to music. I could not find a single person who listened to Motown music, or any other Black music for that matter. There was only one exception to this all-white music rule, only one crossover act, and that was Jimi Hendrix. Somehow, this African-American guitar hero had become the only Black musician deemed acceptable by many white suburbanites. As far as I could figure it was because Hendrix's musical style more closely resembled that of white rock performers like Led Zeppelin, the Rolling Stones and Cream than the soul music being performed by most Blacks at the time. My fellow students seemed oblivious to the irony that Black American blues was the primary influence of those white rock groups.

The cultural racism I witnessed in suburban Detroit was part of much broader and deeply-seated racist attitudes. Many whites routinely used derogatory terms as they openly expressed their hatred of Blacks. And any white person who dressed like a "pimp" and listened to Stevie Wonder and other Motown artists was quickly labelled a "n***** lover." Such was my welcome to the United States. Rather than discovering the free-wheeling, open-minded and rebellious culture that Hollywood movies had so often portrayed, I instead encountered a society that in many ways was more conservative, religious and close-minded than the one I had left behind in England.

But the widespread racism that existed in my new environment was the least of my concerns in high school. I was much more preoccupied with the culture shock I personally experienced upon my arrival in Northville, which proved extremely difficult to cope with and made me suddenly feel like the vulnerable and insecure 15-year-old that I was. I'd been part of the in-crowd, or at least on the fringes of it, in Bramhall High School. But I suddenly found myself to be an outsider, a misfit, in my new surroundings. I found it virtually impossible to penetrate the cliques that constituted the social structures in high school life.

Appearing cool and rebellious was relatively easy for me in England. After all, I didn't have a funny accent and I dressed fashionably and listened to the "right" music. And so, in a contradictory manner, I had carved out an identity for myself in Bramhall that involved appearing to be a rebellious youth while simultaneously being accepted by the in-crowd. In actuality, as is the case with many teens, my rebelliousness did not represent anything of substance, such as challenging the dominant political, social and economic structures of British society. Rather, it consisted of listening to music and wearing clothes that annoyed my parents and others of their generation while simultaneously conforming to the attitudes of most of my peers. In short, it was a relatively comfortable form of rebellious behavior that was primarily driven by a seemingly incomprehensible teenage angst.

In Northville, everything changed. I immediately felt like a real rebel in Northville because I appeared to be truly different than my peers—and that terrified me. So I conformed. I began wearing tee-shirts, jeans and sneakers, although I continued to secretly listen to Black music. But no matter how I tried, I still didn't fit in. Consequently, my only friends in school were a couple of other students who were also misfits for various reasons. But my new friends and I had little in common beyond our existence on the margins of high school society. All of this resulted in me experiencing a very uncomfortable dualistic life. On the one hand, I remained defiantly independent and rebellious on the inside. On the other hand, I tried to conform to local peer-driven cultural practices. I dealt with this identity crisis and resulting insecurity by becoming, basically, a loner, who learned to look out for number one by quietly assuming a "me against the world" attitude.

I wasn't aware of it at the time but my personal crisis mirrored the national identity crisis simultaneously being suffered by the United States. The country was still struggling to come to terms with the social upheavals of the 1960s, its defeat in the Vietnam War, and the Watergate scandal and resulting resignation of President Richard Nixon. Given both my personal and the national contexts, I guess it wasn't surprising that I quickly evolved into the quintessential self-absorbed, alienated, apathetic, apolitical, post-Watergate, middle-class, white, teenage American suburbanite.

Despite my apolitical disposition, I found myself in the fall of 1976 working the phones for Jimmy Carter's presidential campaign. My mother and her friend Mary Paul had been hired by the campaign and they succeeded in getting both me and Mary's son Stephen temporary jobs. Carter was the Democratic Party's candidate, although at the time I knew nothing about him, his campaign platform, his party, the Republican Party or US politics in general—nor did I care. Calling potential voters in the weeks prior to the election to urge them to go out to the polls was simply a way for me to earn money. However, the important aspect of this experience for me ended up having nothing to do with money or politics; rather it had to do with initiating my longest-lasting friendship. Stephen, or rather Steve, was almost two years older than me and was also English. He had moved to Northville after living in Toronto for three years, but instead of attending high school upon his arrival in the United States he went to the local community college, primarily to play for the soccer team.

Because Steve was British, loved music and soccer, and was also an outsider, I immediately connected with him and we became fast friends. He was six-feet tall with jet black hair, dark facial features and an overall look reminiscent of Rasputin. He was also an artist, working primarily with charcoal and oil paints, with most of his work at that time consisting of dark and disturbing portraits. In a way, his artwork constituted a morose version of Van Gogh. Steve and I would spend hours hanging out together in the evenings and on weekends in the basement of his parents' house listening to Alice Cooper and Pink Floyd records. Steve proved to be my social, or rather anti-social, escape from the conformity of high school life. We would often drink beer and occasionally venture outdoors in an attempt to meet girls. Ultimately though, we were far more successful at drinking and listening to music than we were at romance.

In truth, my love life in the "New World" was non-existent. Apparently, the girls at Northville High School had no interest in dating a funny-sounding foreigner. Consequently, I was happy to return to England for a vacation to see Shona and resuscitate my rapidly plummeting levels of self-esteem. My father and I flew from

Detroit to London and he went on to Coventry to meet up with my mother, Don and Karyn, who'd arrived a week earlier. I planned to meet Shona and then rendezvous with my family in Coventry the following evening. I took the train from London to nearby Tonbridge Wells, where she and her family had moved a year earlier. I was filled with anticipation as I pulled into the station and saw Shona standing on the platform. She looked as beautiful as I remembered her from eighteen months earlier. I disembarked and we hugged and kissed. But wait! It wasn't the deep, passionate French kiss that one would expect between two long-lost lovers. Instead, it was, well, a peck on the cheek. Or rather, it consisted of her lips very briefly pecking my cheek. It was a little unnerving to say the least, and on the walk to her parents' house I learned the reason. She had been seeing someone else for the past six months and, apparently, was in love with him. She apologized for not telling me in her letters, admitting that she should have. No shit!

So we arrived at her parents' house and I felt not only uncomfortable, but like a total buffoon. And, as if she hadn't humiliated me enough, Shona then told me that she was going out with her boyfriend that evening and I was more than welcome to join them. What? More than welcome to join them! You mean to say you couldn't even set aside this one evening to spend with me? Don't you think that is the least you could do under the circumstances? Shona maintained that frightfully reserved British air the entire time and I stood there simply dumbfounded. I declined the invitation and, in a desperate attempt to retain what modicum of my dignity that remained, told her that I would catch the train back into London and spend the evening there.

THE EARLY YEARS

Shona and her family were expecting me to return to sleep at their house but I just couldn't bring myself to endure any more humiliation. I didn't have enough money for a hotel so I wandered the streets and explored the city before finally crashing at three o'clock in the morning on a pile of newspapers in Piccadilly Station. It wasn't exactly the romantic reunion with my one true love that I'd been anticipating for months. Devastated, humiliated and with my self-esteem at an all-time low, I returned to the United States two weeks later, not to come to terms with my lonely reality, but to begin years of running away from it.

CHAPTER 2

The Few, the Proud, and the Ugly

My first serious political act as an adult, although I didn't view it that way at the time, was joining the US Marines at nineteen. Not long after graduating from high school I had decided to flee Michigan. I'd briefly attended university on a soccer scholarship, but detested college as much as I'd hated high school. So after I blew out my knee during my first season, and having spent most of my class time in the campus game room, I dropped out. My parents weren't ecstatic about my decision, but not surprised either given my track record at school. As a young man who was finally free to do anything I wanted with my life, I decided to heed the immortal words of Horace Greeley and "Go West."

I drove across the country to a soundtrack consisting of Bruce Springsteen, Bob Dylan, Elvis Costello and Graham Parker and arrived in Los Angeles in the spring of 1979. After two months of sleeping in my car and doing odd jobs in order to survive, I eventually saved enough money to get an apartment. But six months after moving to Los Angeles, the novelty of the city had worn off. There was something depressing about its massive suburban sprawl and its hyper-dependence on the automobile. Los

Angeles, at that time, seemed to be experiencing an identity crisis as the free love hippies of the 1960s and early 1970s were slowly transitioning into the Beamer-driving, mutual fund-trading yuppies of the 1980s. I was becoming restless and desirous of new adventures in new places. The thought of obtaining steady work or a career didn't appeal to me at all because I couldn't think of a single job that I felt passionate about doing. I felt that my life had no purpose. Consequently, I felt lost, bored and in constant need of new stimulation. The unpredictable nature of my work, however, made it difficult to save enough money to hit the road. So, in October 1979, I joined the US Marines.

My enlistment wasn't motivated by any form of patriotism, or even a desire to use the armed forces as a vehicle to obtaining an education, at least not a formal one. I joined because it was an inexpensive path to new adventures overseas in some exotic country. Initially, I was surprised to find that the US military even wanted me. After all, I wasn't a citizen. Evidently, the United States is willing to accept anyone into the military that is dumb enough to enlist.

I was under no illusions that the Marines would be easy; I was fully aware that their boot camp and training were far more demanding than the Army's, which is why they're viewed as a more elite fighting force. Because of my competitive spirit, I actually wanted the toughest branch of the service and the corresponding physical and psychological challenges. At the same time, I had no idea what Marine Corps life would consist of.

I was transported by bus along with a bunch of other new recruits, or "newbies," from downtown Los Angeles to the Marine Corps Recruit Depot in San Diego. The psychological training, or perhaps torture would be a more accurate term, began the moment we stepped off the bus. Marine sergeants immediately began yelling at us, welcoming us to our own "living hell." The first stop was the base's barber shop and within thirty minutes of arriving our heads had been shaved and we were attired in camouflage combat fatigues. We were stripped of not only our hair and clothes, but also of our Christian names and individuality. From that point on, my drill instructors referred to me simply as "Private," or Private Leech on the rare occasion I was to be shown any semblance of respect. I wondered what the hell I'd gotten myself into.

I was assigned to a platoon and shown, along with fifty-nine other newbies, to my new home. The squad bay, or barracks, consisted of a long mostly-barren room with a row of bunk beds down each side, a small office at one end for the drill instructors, and a door leading to the toilets and showers. The first half of Stanley Kubrick's war movie *Full Metal Jacket* accurately captured the intensity and stress of Marine Corps boot camp. What it failed to convey was the full magnitude of the relentlessness of that stress due to its existing day-in and day-out for three months. We did not have a single day off! And the drill instructors made every aspect of our daily routine stressful.

The typical day would begin at 5:30 a.m. with a drill sergeant throwing an empty aluminum trash can the length of the barracks, causing it to bounce down the tile floor. The noise was not only unbelievably loud, it was startling to someone in a deep sleep at the time; and I had never slept as deeply as I did during that three months due to being so physically and mentally exhausted at the end of each day. We were expected to immediately jump up out of bed and, attired only in the white tee-shirts and boxer shorts that constituted our regulation sleeping attire, stand at attention at the end of our bunks. We were then given two minutes to go to the toilet and return to our positions at the end of our bunks. Given that there were sixty of us, it often amounted to an impossible task. And when we didn't meet our deadline we would be collectively punished by the drill sergeant. We were ordered to hit the deck and perform various calisthenics such as push-ups, jumping jacks, sit-ups, squat thrusts and leg-lifts while a drill instructor screamed at us.

The high level of tension was maintained throughout the day; in fact, everything we did was done under duress. We were forced to either run or to march everywhere we went, we were never allowed to just walk. We ran to the bathroom. We ran from the barracks to outdoors. We ran from outdoors into the barracks. We ran or marched in formation to exercise areas or to the classrooms. We ran or marched in formation to the mess hall. Often at meal times we were told that we were going to eat duck. This didn't mean that we were about to ingest that particular form of fowl, but rather that we were going to "duck" into the mess hall, grab our food, eat it and "duck" back out, all in five minutes.

Our physical training took place in the mornings and involved running, calisthenics, hand-to-hand combat and tackling a variety of obstacle courses, including rappelling towers. Afternoons were spent in classrooms where we were educated, or rather indoctrinated, in the glory of the Marine Corps' history and that of the wonderful country it was our destiny to defend. Not surprisingly, there was no critical analysis of any of these historical events. In fact, it was like a super-intense version of a high school history class. We also studied practical things, at least from a military point of view, such as how to assemble, disassemble and clean an M-16 semi-automatic assault rifle. For two weeks in the middle of boot camp we relocated to Camp Pendleton, a Marine Corps base just up the Pacific Coast, to engage in rifle and infantry training. This is where we learned to shoot our weapons and to haul sixty-pound backpacks up and down mountains all day long while being bombarded with insults.

Throughout boot camp our after-dinner routine consisted of returning to the squad bay where our drill sergeants instructed us on Marine Corps etiquette and other little nuggets of information intended to help us be better "Jarheads," as Marines are nicknamed. We were given one hour of free time at 8:30 p.m. during which we had to remain in the barracks. This was the only time of the day that we were allowed to speak, or rather whisper, to each other. Free time was also when we could shower and shave, as well as read and write letters. For three months those letters represented our only contact with the outside world. We were not allowed to watch television or listen to the radio, and there were no reading materials such as newspapers, magazines or books permitted. We lived in virtual isolation.

The objective of the constant abuse was to eradicate to the greatest degree possible any individuality in each recruit, to ensure that they could endure high levels of stress and, ultimately, to create an obedient military robot, or killing machine, who bled Marine Corps green and would never question anything, particularly orders from higher-ranking Marines.

I graduated from boot camp in January 1980 feeling indestructible and began six weeks at Infantry Training School in Camp Pendleton where I learned to be an anti-tank assault man. The job required learning to fire LAWs rockets, or Light Anti-Tank Weapons, in order to disable tanks and how to use plastic explosives and set charges. One of the principal purposes for learning to use explosives was to take out enemy bunkers. Since the Marines were the first to hit the beaches, they were required to destroy those fortifications from which the enemy could easily pick-off our troops as they landed. As was exhibited in countless John Wayne war movies, some poor sucker would race up a hill towards an enemy bunker with a satchel full of explosives in his hand. If he succeeded in dodging the constant stream of enemy bullets aimed at him, he would toss the satchel through the opening of the bunker and heroically eliminate the threat. Basically, it was a suicide mission. And so, for six weeks, I learned how to blow things up.

Upon completing Infantry Training School I received the overseas posting that I had desired. In March 1980, I was deployed to Panama, which was my first experience in a tropical Third World country. And while I experienced a degree of culture shock, it was dramatically diminished by my being there as a Marine. The Marine Corps mission in Panama was to guard US Naval installations, which included a base, a fuel depot and several communications centers on both the Pacific and Caribbean coasts of the country. The Marines and Navy did not constitute the entire US military presence in Panama, as both the Air Force and Army also maintained bases there. In fact, there were more than 10,000 US troops permanently based in the country. They were stationed at various locations along the Panama Canal. The protection of the canal was the principal mission of the US military, and the Canal Zone, which paralleled the canal on either side, had constituted a little strip of US territory in Panama for most of the 20th century.

The United States had opportunistically seized the strip of land that effectively cut Panama in half in 1902 when the country seceded from Colombia. US gunboats had ensured that the Colombian military didn't squelch the secessionist uprising in Panama and in return Washington helped itself to a portion of the new nation in order to build the transoceanic canal. More than five thousand laborers died building the canal, but that wasn't seen as a major problem because it wasn't Americans doing the dying; it was mostly poor Black workers imported from Caribbean islands.

During those decades the United States made a habit of using its gunboat diplomacy to steal pieces of land from other countries. It constituted a new form of colonialism in which acquiring a small strategically important piece of land within a country was easier than trying to directly rule an entire nation full of restless natives. This was precisely how we obtained the Guantanamo Bay Naval Base in Cuba, which we have most recently used as an internment camp in the war on terror.

The difference between the standard of living in the Canal Zone and that in most of Panama City, which was situated directly adjacent to the Canal Zone, was startling. It was possible to travel from the First World to the Third World by simply crossing the street. The presence of so many US military personnel and their families also heavily influenced the culture of Panama City. I didn't realize at the time just how arrogant and superior the attitudes of many military personnel were towards the Panamanian people. It was an imperial arrogance at a personal level that reflected the imperial arrogance of a nation that believed it had the right to station its military anywhere in the world while never permitting troops from a foreign country to be based on US soil. But I was not conscious of this reality at the time; I had no interest in politics. Consequently, I exhibited the same arrogant attitude toward Panamanians as my colleagues.

Many aspects of the city, particularly the nightlife, were geared towards attracting off-duty US troops. And at nineteen years of age it was the nightlife and, more specifically, the Panamanian women that appealed to me. There were no shortage of Panamanian women who hung out in the discotheques and bars seeking companionship with US troops. They saw us as their tickets out of poverty, either temporarily by hooking up with a serviceman for the length of his tour of duty in Panama or permanently through marriage.

In contrast to the excitement of the nightlife in Panama City was the monotony of our daily routine on base. My military activities mostly involved hours upon tedious hours of guard duty, painting palm trees for some unknown reason, cleaning already spotless rifles, participating in litter detail, and many other mind-numbing, time-filling chores. There was only one military experience during my posting in Panama that I found at all stimulating. It occurred when our unit travelled to an army base on the Caribbean coast to attend the US Army Special Forces' Jungle Warfare Training Program at the School of the Americas. We learned how to survive in, and how to navigate our way through, the jungle. The final phase of the program involved small groups of us being deployed into the jungle and having to navigate our way to a specific rendezvous point. I volunteered to be point man and hacking my way through the rainforest with a machete was the most meaningful experience I had in Panama. In a strange way, I felt comfortable and relaxed, I even felt at home. After all, it encapsulated what I most wanted at that point in my life: new experiences and adventure.

As the months passed I grew to detest the dehumanizing, desensitizing and tedious nature of military life. I found it supremely ironic that an institution charged with defending democracy and its related individual freedoms, particularly the freedom of expression, was so reliant on squelching those very freedoms in order to function. Furthermore, it seemed that the hierarchical structure of the Marine Corps not only gave those of superior rank the right to give orders, but to also treat those below them as sub-human. In fact, the prestige of non-commissioned officers appeared to rest on their ability to abuse subordinates. Furthermore, with the challenges posed by Boot Camp and Infantry Training School behind me, life in the Marines was no longer proving to be an adventure. In short, it was boring. I'd had enough and wanted out; and so I became increasingly disobedient of my superiors.

I began missing guard duty by not returning to base in time for assignments. Sometimes I'd be gone for two or three days and would finally return when my money ran out. Eventually, I just began blatantly refusing to follow orders. These offenses resulted in my being demoted from Lance-Corporal, the highest rank I achieved before I began rebelling, down to Private First-Class and, ultimately, back to Private. The punishments imposed on me also included being restricted to base for set periods of time. When I ignored those disciplinary rulings and continued to leave base and miss duty assignments, I was unceremoniously dispatched to the brig at the US Army's Fort Clayton.

THE FEW, THE PROUD, AND THE UGLY

I spent thirty-five days in a jail cell. It was supposed to be punishment, but it wasn't. I actually found incarceration preferable to my normal duties. It was no more tedious or dehumanizing than routine Marine Corps life and, in some ways, I had more autonomy. For instance, I had access to books from the base library and could spend hours upon hours in my cell each day peacefully reading escapist fare such as mystery and crime novels. Upon realizing that the stint in the brig was not going to curb my insolence, the commanding officer of the Marine detachment in Panama offered me a general discharge for, as he clearly stated, "the good of the service." Naturally, I immediately accepted his offer, for the good of me.

I left Panama in March 1981 detesting Marine Corps life but having become curious about Latin America. There was something exotic and fascinating about the region's jungles, people and culture. I flew back to the United States to be processed out of the Marines at Parris Island in South Carolina, after which I returned home to Michigan. I knew that I would head back to Latin America soon. What I didn't know was that my next visit to the region would constitute the beginning of my long, slow political awakening. But first, there would be a serious flirtation with Ayn Rand.

CHAPTER 3

My Salvadoran Nightmare

Upon my discharge from the Marines I was left to reflect on my life and my future. I was feeling depressed and disenchanted. I'd hated high school, dropped out of university and been kicked out of the Marines. I wondered whether I'd ever feel passionate about anything; or if I would find anywhere that I belonged. The only time I felt remotely happy was when I was experiencing new adventures. But they always proved short lived. And no matter what I did or where I went, I still felt like an outsider, a misfit. My rebellious nature had come to the fore, but I didn't know what I was rebelling against, never mind what I was fighting for. I was desperately seeking some sort of meaning to my life but had no idea how to find it. Such was my state of mind when I returned home to visit my family in Northville after being discharged from the Marines. After spending a few days with my family, I packed my bags again and headed to the nearby city of Ann Arbor to live with Steve while I pondered the quintessential question of youth: "What am I going to do with my life?"

Steve and I had stayed in touch during my years away from the Detroit area and he remained my closest friend. In actuality, he was my only real friend. Steve was working in a liquor store two blocks from the apartment in which he lived with an ex-girlfriend named Laura. They had the top two floors of an old three-story house, which included a spare bedroom. I lived with Steve and Laura until the end of the summer. I suppose some might call it a lost summer due to the amount of cocaine, hallucinogenic mushrooms and beer we consumed during that four-month period, but we had a lot of fun. Steve was cocky, opinionated and had a façade of self-confidence that masked the insecurity common among males in their early twenties. He also had a sharp wit; a scathingly sarcastic sense of humor.

Our lives had gone in dramatically different directions since my school days in Northville. While most of my journey had involved a variety of physical geographies, Steve's had been a much more philosophical odyssey. He'd left home at eighteen and moved in with an older woman. When that relationship ended, he enrolled at the University of Michigan to study art. Disenchanted with the academic approach to the subject, he dropped out and focused on his own artwork and broader questions about life while working at the liquor store.

Despite the amount of partying that occurred during that summer, or dare I say because of it, those months with Steve actually helped me to begin re-orienting myself, at least to the degree that I was capable of at that point in my life. That period represented my first serious effort to engage in philosophical reflection. Steve introduced me to the work of an author who had an immediate and significant impact on me. Her name was Ayn Rand and her philosophical ideas fell under the moniker Objectivism, which constituted a form of libertarianism. Rand had emigrated from the Soviet Union in the early 1920s as a young woman. She reached the United States and became an ardent advocate of laissez-faire capitalism. In fact, she was a libertarian who valued individual responsibility, rationality, competition and selfishness above everything else. Rand's personal philosophy was dominated by individualism to the extreme, advocating complete self-reliance, or what she called "selfishness," to the degree that feeling any compassion for another human being's frailties was considered to be a character flaw. When asked if it was immoral for people to prioritize friends and family, Rand responded by stating that if people "place such things as friendship and family ties above their own productive work, yes, then they are immoral. Friendship, family life and human relationships are not primary in a man's life." Naturally, the flip-side of this lack of compassion for fellow beings was the capacity to judge them.

Given that I was emotionally repressed due to my British upbringing and my Marine Corps indoctrination; had felt like an outsider for years with no sense of community; possessed a competitive spirit; and woke up each day feeling as though it was me against the world, Rand's purely rationally-based, emotion-less, competitive, individualistic philosophy not only resonated with me, it actually made me feel empowered. I even felt enlightened, albeit in the same delusionary way that a member of the Klu Klux Klan or an anti-gay religious conservative feels enlightened by the narrative of their particular community. I finally had affirmation of my affinity for functioning almost entirely as a rational being, and justification for repressing my emotional side. It also allowed me to feel morally superior to others and to become even more judgmental of those around me and of society in general. In short, it gave me an identity. And, disturbingly, it made me even more arrogant.

Rand's philosophy fit nicely with the conservative vision of the American Dream. It reflected many of the values espoused by Ronald Reagan, who was president at the time. First and foremost among those values was the trumpeting of the culture of individualism. After all, if one was willing to work hard then there was no reason one couldn't get ahead in life, right? Anything was possible if a person put their mind to it. Correspondingly, if a person fails, it's due to their own shortcomings such as laziness, stupidity, naiveté or some other individual flaw. This "rational selfishness" was expressed by Rand as "Man—every man—is an end in himself, not the means to the ends of others. ... The pursuit of his own rational self-interest and of his own happiness is the highest moral purpose of his life."

I devoured Rand's books, both fiction and non-fiction. I was completely captivated by her philosophical views on the individual and society. After all, I believed I'd already exhibited an ability to survive a variety of environments thanks to my own initiative and individualism. I suddenly believed that the alienation I'd felt for years wasn't a negative; it was actually a source of strength. My ability to cope with that alienation and other adversities had simply strengthened me as an individual. I remained oblivious to the fact that my capacity to overcome challenges through initiative and individualism was largely due to the unearned privilege that comes with being a white middle-class male. In short, the Objectivist philosophy seemed like common sense to me.

At the end of that summer of debauchery and reflection I got a job in the meat department of a supermarket located in the Detroit suburb of South Lyon. My objective was to save enough money to return to Latin America. My brother Don, who had completed one year of university in Arizona before dropping out and returning to Michigan, wasn't sure what he wanted to do with his life. He thought a little adventure sounded like a good idea and decided to join me on the trip. Don and I were very different, both physically and personality wise. I was six-feet-one-inch tall with dark brown hair. I was also cocky and self-absorbed, not having the time of day for other people unless they served a specific purpose. Don was five-feet-nine with light brown hair and was far more introverted than me. Throughout his youth he'd been fascinated with history and was an avid reader of academic texts far in advance of his age. Not surprisingly, he would go on to become a history professor.

Don and I set off on our adventure in December 1981, travelling as cheaply as possible so as to make our journey last. Our vague objective was to travel by land from Detroit to Panama, primarily by hitch-hiking and taking buses. It would mark the beginning of more than a year of non-stop wandering for me as I continued to search for my place in the world. Ayn Rand had helped provide me with a philosophical perspective, but I still had no idea about what I wanted do or where I should do it.

Don and I traversed Central America and eventually reached Panama City. After a week there, Don departed and made his own way back home to Detroit. I decided to visit the Darien Gap, which is a rugged, remote region of jungle, swamps and mountains in eastern Panama. Once my money supply had dwindled to an uncomfortably low level, I also left Panama and began my long journey home. I traveled by bus through Costa Rica, Nicaragua and Honduras. In early

MY SALVADORAN NIGHTMARE

March 1982, the old dilapidated but colorfully decorated bus that I was travelling on in Honduras finally reached the border with El Salvador. I maneuvered my way through the typical border chaos and paid the equivalent of two dollars to obtain the necessary exit stamps in my passport. I then set out on foot across the border bridge, arriving a few minutes later at the Salvadoran checkpoint called El Amatillo. It was at this point that things began to get ugly.

A Salvadoran border guard dumped the contents of my backpack onto a table and after sifting through my belongings singled out a book of poetry written by Patti Smith. The border guard flipped through the pages and noticed a black and white picture of the author holding a walkie-talkie. Unable to read English, he assumed it to be revolutionary literature. I tried in vain to convince him otherwise, but after another official noticed my old, beat up, military-looking black boots, they decided to detain me at the border overnight. The following morning, I was placed in handcuffs and transported to a military base in the nearby city of La Unión along with a Nicaraguan woman who had also been detained at the border. Upon arrival, the handcuffs were removed and replaced with a shoelace that tied my thumbs together behind my back. The soldiers sat me on a bench just inside the gate and left me there to stare at the lime green paint peeling slowly off a wall situated two feet in front of my face.

At some point during the afternoon an army officer came to interrogate me and it was then that I discovered the reason for my detainment. I'd been accused of being a mercenary working with the Marxist guerrillas who were fighting to overthrow the Salvadoran government. I answered all of his questions; though needless to say I neglected to mention my military service for fear that it might incriminate me in light of the mercenary accusation. Eventually the officer departed and I was left alone to ponder the fact that I was a suspected mercenary. Still, I managed to remain relatively optimistic, believing they would soon sort out the misunderstanding and set me free.

Shortly after nightfall a group of soldiers came and placed a blindfold over my head. They stood me up and pulled me along by my arms, which proved to be intensely painful for my thumbs, which were still tied together. I struggled to maintain both my calm and my footing as the soldiers led me blindfolded through a maze of unannounced obstacles including stairs and low doorways. Being led blindfolded through that base by soldiers who viewed me as their enemy was absolutely terrifying. At the end of that brief but nerve-wracking trek, the soldiers let go of my arms and pushed me to the floor. I heard footsteps receding and then a door being slammed shut and locked. The blindfold had served its purpose, for I had no idea where I was or how to get out of there.

After a few minutes I began rubbing the side of my head against the stucco wall and successfully removed the blindfold. The room was approximately twelve-by-twelve feet with light blue stucco walls, a red tile floor and no furniture. There was one window with wooden shutters but no glass; it was the source of what little light penetrated the room. There were two doors, the one through which I had entered and another that opened into a bathroom containing a toilet and a brass pipe running up the wall, which was meant to serve as a shower. Lying motionless in the corner of the main room was the Nicaraguan woman who had traveled with me from the border. She was blindfolded with her thumbs tied together behind her back.

I was obviously there for the night and was concerned with the fact that my situation seemed to be deteriorating with each passing moment. Still, I did my best to convince myself that I would soon be free once they checked out the information I'd given them that afternoon. I tried to get some sleep but it was impossible to find a comfortable position on the hard tile floor. Lying on either side, or on my back, soon put my arms to sleep. And lying on my stomach only caused me pain due to the weight of my arms pulling my thumbs apart and causing the ties to cut into the skin. I spent the night sitting upright in the corner where I drifted in and out of sleep.

The following morning three soldiers brought us breakfast and, to my relief, were unconcerned with the fact that I was no longer blindfolded. Like most of the soldiers I saw during my detention, they were young men in their late teens. They removed the Nicaraguan woman's blindfold and both of our thumb ties before leaving us alone to eat. After finishing her breakfast the Nicaraguan woman made her way into the bathroom. The three soldiers returned while she was in there. Upon realizing where she was, they retied my thumbs and disappeared through the bathroom door. I heard muffled female cries and male laughter from behind that closed door, leaving little doubt about what was taking place. I felt so helpless sitting there with my thumbs tied while they raped that defenseless woman. I thought of shouting for help but realized that it might only result in more soldiers joining in on the abuse. I felt sick to my stomach.

After a while the three soldiers emerged laughing from the bathroom, obviously full of themselves. They picked up our breakfast dishes and left. Through the open bathroom door I could hear the woman sobbing and was undecided whether or not to go in there. I was not sure whether my presence would bring her comfort or just instill more fear in her. I decided to leave her alone; perhaps more for me than for her. A couple of hours later she emerged from the bathroom and settled back into her corner. When I asked her if she was all right, she ignored me. She was as alone and terrified as any person I had ever seen and I felt that there was nothing I could do to help her. Thankfully, for the remainder of the time that I spent with her, she was only subjected to verbal taunting, which she endured in silence.

Over the next couple of days I was interrogated two more times by different officers. I repeatedly requested in vain to speak with the British Embassy. Even though I'd lived in the United States for six years and had served in the Marines, I had yet to become a US citizen and was, therefore, still British. I knew that the Salvadoran government was legally required to notify the embassy of any British citizen they arrested, and the growing realization that they had no intention of doing so made me suddenly feel very isolated. I had last contacted my family when I was in Nicaragua and all they knew was that I was somewhere between Nicaragua and the United States. Meanwhile, the Nicaraguan woman continued to ignore any attempt I made to communicate with her. I never did learn her name. In fact, she never uttered a single word to me during our time together.

On the third morning of my detention I heard raised voices from outside the room. Peering through the shutters, I saw a naked man who appeared to be in his twenties performing calisthenics in the dirt courtyard. Soldiers stood on both sides of him and, every time that he failed to perform up to their expectations, they beat him with sticks.

Cheered on by their comrades, they whipped him until tears streamed down his face and blood down his back. Eventually the semi-conscious man was carried from the courtyard and taken into what appeared to be a room similar to ours.

I wondered if at some point I was going to have to endure a similar punishment. But in spite of having just observed both that senseless abuse and the rape of the Nicaraguan woman, I still thought it inconceivable that such a thing could happen to me. My attitude was undoubtedly influenced, rather naively, by the belief that they would never subject a foreigner who lived in the United States to such treatment. After all, I reassured myself, the United States was their ally. At that time, all I knew about the Salvadoran Civil War was that the United States supported the Salvadoran army in its battle against Marxist guerrillas. Having been thoroughly socialized to believe that Western democracies, particularly the US and British models, represented all that was good in the world, I logically assumed that the US-backed Salvadoran army must therefore represent the force for good in that war.

My fourth day began with the usual breakfast of rice, beans and a tortilla, but shortly afterwards a group of soldiers came for me. My thumbs were again tied together behind my back and a blindfold placed over my eyes. I was led out of the room and after a few minutes walked into something solid, which I quickly determined to be the open tailgate of a pick-up truck. I was pulled up, to a large extent by my hair, onto the bed of the truck and forced to lie down amongst other live bodies. It was creepy lying on top of the wriggling bodies of people I could not see and who were most likely in the same predicament as myself. Who were they? What had they done? What will happen to them?

What will happen to all of us? There was a short drive that terminated next to the deafening sound of a helicopter. I was pulled out of the truck and, amid the nerve-wracking noise and commotion, stumbled into some steps. My guards again pulled me up by my hair, this time into the helicopter. Once aboard I was pushed down to the floor where I lay on my stomach next to the other prisoners. The helicopter took off and we remained airborne for about thirty minutes. During the flight I suddenly felt a sharp pain in my left ear. A soldier had just ripped out my gold hoop earring.

When we landed I was placed into the rear of a van. Following a very short drive, I was pulled out of the van and the thumb ties were replaced with handcuffs. When I stumbled climbing some steps, one of my guards began beating me with what I assumed to be his rifle butt. Most of the blows struck me on the right hipbone, causing me to wince in pain and to curse at the soldier in English. While it is doubtful that he understood the words, he certainly recognized the tone, which only caused him to intensify the beating. My response was stupid, but it represented an impulsive and desperate attempt to gain some control over my situation.

I was deposited in a large warehouse and interrogated yet again. Afterwards, a soldier put the blindfold back on and led me out of the building. After a short walk I came to a halt and the blindfold was removed. I found myself standing inside a barred gate with a twelve-foot high wall on my left and opposite it, to my right, were three jail cells. The barred door to the third cell was unlocked and opened and, after my handcuffs had been removed, I was placed inside. The cell was approximately twelve-by-fifteen feet with gray cement walls. There was a built-in cement seat running around the walls and a ceiling of steel bars that hung several feet below the roof. In one corner were the now familiar brass pipe shower and a white porcelain toilet without a seat. The cell was occupied by ten Latino men, all of whom seemed surprised to discover that their new cellmate was a gringo.

Entering that cell I envisioned all kinds of horrors, but my fears were soon alleviated when most of my new cellmates displayed nothing but friendliness towards me. One of my fellow prisoners was a 20-year-old university student named Carlos who claimed to have been arrested, along with two friends, for drinking in a parked car outside the international airport one evening. With the aid of a Spanish language *Reader's Digest*, which Carlos had somehow managed to procure, the two of us spent much of the next three days giving each other Spanish and English lessons. Most of the other prisoners also claimed to be students who'd been arrested for trivial reasons, although there were two prisoners who were unwilling to share their stories and who kept mostly to themselves.

I discovered that I was in the capital, San Salvador. Over the next few days I learned that my Spanish teacher had been in jail for over a month and had not seen his friends since the night of their arrest. Also, he had not been allowed to contact his family who, as far as he knew, remained unaware of his predicament. Both of his thumbs had ugly red wounds about a quarter of an inch deep where ties had literally cut through his skin. It was several months before I regained the full feeling in my thumbs, so it was hard to imagine him not suffering permanent damage.

There was barely enough room in the cell for all of us to lie down and sleep on the cement floor, which in the early hours of the morning became uncomfortably cold.

The blue tank-top and beige cotton pants I'd been wearing since my arrest offered little in the way of warmth. Each meal consisted of rice, beans and a tortilla, and as the days passed I began to lose my appetite. Whether this was due to worry or inactivity I'm not entirely sure, but the other prisoners were happy recipients of my leftovers.

Our showers had to be taken during the morning hours due to the fact that there was no drain and the flooded floor, which also served as our bed, required most of the day to dry. It was when they showered that I noticed several of my cellmates wore brutal looking scars across their backs, undoubtedly a result of beatings similar to the one I had witnessed in La Unión. For me though, the most unpleasant aspect of life in that cell was the fact that eleven men were using a toilet that had no real flushing mechanism. We would fill an empty coffee can with water from the shower and wash the waste down the toilet as best we could. At first, the daytime heat and humidity made the stench unbearable, but to my amazement its oppressiveness diminished with each passing day as I became accustomed to the foul odor.

The next three days passed without any further interrogations and the time dragged. Boredom and increasing concern became the dominant factors in my detention. I could see no way out of my predicament and a new fear emerged. It wasn't a fear of being physically hurt, but rather a fear of the psychological torture that would inevitably result from a prolonged imprisonment. I also couldn't stop thinking about my parents and the endless torment they would have to endure once they realized that I'd gone missing.

Late in the afternoon of the seventh day, my salvation arrived in the form of the International Committee of the

Red Cross. Several Red Cross workers were engaging in a random inspection of the jail and were very surprised to find a gringo prisoner. After relating my story to them I was informed that they didn't have the authority to get me released, but they would notify the British Consulate of my situation. They then turned their attention to the other prisoners and, to my amazement, not one of my cellmates registered a complaint about their predicament or their treatment. These were people who had been victims of abuses resulting in crippled thumbs, brutally scarred backs and who knows what else. As if that were not bad enough, they had no doubt also endured psychological torment and been denied any form of contact with the outside world, including their families. After the Red Cross workers departed, I asked Carlos why none of them had spoken out about their treatment.

"If we complain there will be repercussions against us and our families," he explained.

He then went on to reassure me that, because I was a foreigner, the Red Cross visit would most likely result in my release. This news left me feeling truly optimistic for the first time in almost a week, and yet a little uncomfortable with the favorable treatment I appeared to be receiving.

Carlos was proved right the next morning when two guards came to take me away. I hastily bid farewell to my cellmates. As I left with the guards, who this time did not blindfold me, I was overcome with a strange mixture of sadness and relief. I wondered what lay in store for Carlos and the others I was leaving behind, and could not avoid feeling guilty about the fact that my government had the power to gain my release, whereas their government was the party responsible for their dilemma.

The guards led me through the outer cell gate and across a large open courtyard to a small office building. A Salvadoran army officer was seated at a desk in one of the offices. A very British-looking elderly gentleman sat across from him. The officer introduced the man to me as Mr. William Chippendale, the British Honorary Consul. The officer then handed me my backpack, my passport and, to my surprise, my money. However, the Patti Smith book and the poetry that I had written during my travels were not among my belongings. Chippendale suggested that I not make an issue of the missing items if I wished to get out of there in the near future. Needless to say I took his advice. The Salvadoran officer told me I was free to go on the condition that I leave the country immediately and never return. It was a condition I gladly accepted.

The consul and I left the office and made our way to the front gate of the base. I cannot describe the overwhelming sense of relief that I experienced as we walked through that gate and out onto the street. I inhaled, what seemed to me, the freshest air on the planet. We then climbed into Chippendale's car and he explained that he'd not known of my existence until the Red Cross had contacted him earlier that morning. He then asked me a few questions about my ordeal and said that he would be filing an official protest regarding the fact that the Salvadoran authorities had failed to notify him of my arrest. The honorary consul then drove me to the bus station where I thanked him and boarded a bus to the Guatemalan border. I didn't fully realize it at the time, but for eight days I had experienced a minuscule amount of the terror that many Salvadorans endured for more than a decade. I was lucky to get out of there alive; more than seventy thousand Salvadorans were not.

CHAPTER 4

Tying and Untying the Knot

For the second time in twelve months I was returning home from Latin America having endured a traumatic experience. On the first occasion, it had been my battle to liberate myself from the drudgery and de-humanizing nature of life in the Marines. In the latter instance, it was my imprisonment in El Salvador. When I saw Steve upon my return he asked, "What the fuck were you thinking hitchhiking through a war zone?" Of course, he had a point. For that matter, what the fuck was I thinking with regard to most of the things I'd done in my life? But for me, the way I approached life had nothing to do with a death wish and everything to do with the fact that new experiences and adventures were the only things that made me feel alive.

But how is one supposed to cope with the trauma that results from the sort of ordeal I'd just endured in El Salvador? One seemingly obvious response would be to become politicized and learn more about what was going on in that troubled nation. Then perhaps one could work in solidarity with those Salvadorans whose human rights were being violated. Of course, that's not how I responded. No self-respecting, self-absorbed, Ayn Rand-loving individualist would respond that way. After all, we are each only responsible for ourselves, right? So I responded by, well, not responding at all. I simply buried any trauma resulting from the experience deep down in my psyche and continued running from myself.

I spent the next six months aimlessly hitchhiking around the United States before returning to Detroit where I got a job working as a butcher in a suburban supermarket. During my first year on the job I met a cashier named Elizabeth and we began dating. Elizabeth, at twenty years of age, was four years younger than me. Her parents had moved to the Detroit area from Kentucky in the early 1960s so her father could avoid a life spent in the coal mines by working in an automobile factory instead. She was young and incredibly naïve, as was I when it came to relationships. She had lived in the same house for her entire life. She had never travelled, beyond visiting family in Kentucky. She was responsible and desired little more than a stable, secure existence with a loving husband. In short, Elizabeth was everything that I wasn't.

We got married in 1985 and made our home in a trailer park in the Detroit suburb of Novi. Had I finally settled down to a life of bliss? It seemed so to me. Because I was tired of my vagabond existence and frustrated at the lack of purpose in my life, a sedentary lifestyle with a steady job and a stable relationship held a certain appeal for me at that point in time. And so began my attempt at living a more conventional life in the US Midwest. After a hard and bloody day spent cutting up animal carcasses, I would head home for dinner and an evening watching television with my wife. But I soon became depressed and frustrated with my life, and I responded by turning to a longtime passion:

music. But instead of just listening to it, I decided to fulfill a teenage fantasy and teach myself guitar so that I could write songs. At the age of twenty-six, I had finally found something that I was passionate about doing. I was serious about something for the first time ever. Music became my escape from my unhappy existence.

This period was also marked by a growing political awareness on my part. Two things occurred in the mid-1980s that began to influence my worldview: a growing desire to finally reflect on my El Salvador experience and my father suffering a serious heart attack. The relative security provided by my conventional life in the Midwest and the passage of time allowed me to finally begin reflecting on my Salvadoran nightmare. My reflections were triggered by a movie I watched titled *Salvador*, which was directed by Oliver Stone and starred James Woods. Shortly afterwards, the movie *Romero* would also have a profound impact on me. That movie focused on the life of Archbishop Oscar Romero, who was assassinated in March 1980 by former Salvadoran soldiers trained by the US military. He was murdered because he had been using his pulpit to plead with Salvadoran soldiers to stop killing their brothers and sisters. Those two movies shed light on the brutality of the Salvadoran military and inspired me to begin reading articles and books about that country's civil war.

I began to learn about the gross violations of human rights perpetrated by the US-backed Salvadoran military against both Salvadorans and foreigners. I learned how members of the Salvadoran military brutally raped and murdered four female missionaries from the United States in 1980. In December 1981, troops from the Salvadoran army's elite Atlacatl Battalion, which was created, funded, trained and armed by the United States, massacred more than nine hundred peasants in and around the village of El Mozote. Most of the victims were women and children. The army executed four foreign journalists the following year. The list of atrocities perpetrated by the US-backed Salvadoran military was extensive and would continue to the end of the decade when US-trained soldiers massacred six Jesuit priests, their housekeeper and her 16-year-old daughter.

I had personally witnessed a minuscule amount of that terror during my detention in El Salvador and was now beginning to understand the real plight faced by Carlos and my other cellmates. I also understood that there was a good chance none of them were still alive, and that realization left me feeling horribly guilty. I hadn't fully realized at the time of my release from prison just how lucky I was to have gotten out of there alive. I also hadn't realized during the years following my release that I was dealing with my survivor guilt by sub-consciously denying both the reality of what I had witnessed and the role played by my government. This disassociation had been made easier by my adherence to Ayn Rand's philosophy of individualism.

Rather than responding to my experience with compassion for my fellow prisoners and a desire to better understand the human rights situation in El Salvador, I had instead become increasingly isolated and even more emotionally repressed. But by 1986 I was beginning to realize that what might have seemed like a perfectly logical response for a self-absorbed person like me was not necessarily a healthy one. I was starting to understand that my outward persona of a cocky and conceited young man was merely a façade that concealed an incredibly insecure human being desperately struggling to find his place in the world. I was finally engaging in serious self-reflection. I was no longer running away; I was honestly trying to understand myself.

My privileged, apolitical, white, middle-class upbringing meant that I had been indoctrinated with the dominant ideological perspective of my culture, which posited that free-market capitalism, Western liberal democracy and the culture of individualism represented freedom, progress and a force for good in the world. In this context, my attraction to Ayn Rand made perfect sense, since it reinforced and validated the belief system and many of the values that I'd internalized. But cracks were now appearing in the structures of my belief system following my discovery that the US role in El Salvador was linked to gross violations of human rights in the name of defending democracy, freedom and capitalism. In other words, in the name of defending the values that I believed in.

My worldview was also shaken in 1987 when my father suffered a heart attack. He'd worked for the multinational tractor manufacturer Massey Ferguson in England for seventeen years before being transferred to the United States. He worked for the company there for seven more years before being transferred again, this time to Canada. His heart attack, which almost killed him, occurred while he was living in Canada and his recovery kept him off work for several months. Shortly after returning to work he was laid off along with hundreds of others. At fifty-four years of age, and after more than twenty-eight years of dedicated and loyal service to Massey Ferguson, the company had fired him; not because he could no longer do his job, but to generate greater profits for its shareholders.

Massey Ferguson had obtained a $200 million bailout from the Canadian government in the early 1980s in return for promising to maintain its head office and a specified number of employees in Canada. Several years later, Massey Ferguson changed the name of its Canadian subsidiary to Varity, which in turn established a new firm named Massey Combines. My father woke up one morning to find that after twenty-eight years he no longer worked for Massey Ferguson; he was now employed by Massey Combines. Massey Combines then declared bankruptcy and all of its Canadian workers were laid off while Varity fled Canada to operate its profitable Massey Ferguson division in the United States. The US-based Massey Ferguson then re-acquired all of the assets of the bankrupt Massey Combines.

Varity only had to pay a $25 million penalty for breaking the company's agreement with the Canadian government and another $27 million in severance pay and medical benefits to its former Canadian employees. The company only made the latter payment after spending three years fighting a class action suit brought against it by the fired workers. At the end of the day, Varity got to keep $143 million of the taxpayer-funded bailout after declaring its Canadian division bankrupt and then abandoning Canada.

Not only did my father suddenly find himself unemployed, but he also only received 50 percent of his pension. It turned out that he wasn't fully vested because he was still one-and-a-half years short of completing thirty years on the job. To add insult to injury, Varity cut off all medical benefits to its Canadian workers when Massey Combines declared bankruptcy, thereby leaving my father to cover $300 a month in drug prescription bills for his heart condition out of his own pocket. It wasn't until after the class action suit was settled three years later that he regained a portion of his medical coverage.

My father believed, as did many of his generation, that if you exhibited loyalty and dedication to your employer, which he did both at work and by relocating his family to two foreign countries when requested, that it would be reciprocated with job security and a respectable pension upon retirement. The principal exception to this rule throughout much of the 20th century was when a company went bankrupt because it was losing money. But Massey Ferguson wasn't losing money, it cynically shut down its struggling Canadian operations at a time when the company's overall global operations were profitable. Even more troubling was Massey Ferguson's total lack of compassion and sense of fairness toward its workers. Witnessing my father's experience with Massey Ferguson would ultimately have a profound impact upon the way I viewed corporate capitalism.

During these years, songwriting also began to play a significant role in my self-reflection. In many ways it replaced travelling as my vehicle for exploration. Writing songs was an exploration that was much more internally focused. In fact, music was the mechanism through which I became truly introspective for the first time in my life. Reading Ayn Rand had not led me to reflect on myself so much as it had provided me with a convenient philosophical coat that fit comfortably over my insecurities. But songwriting began revealing aspects of myself that I was previously unaware of; things that I'd been in denial about for years.

Songwriting for me was not entirely a conscious process. I would come up with a chord progression and then hum a melody over it. The humming would evolve into words that just emerged from my mouth. I wouldn't think about the words and would write down each verse as it came out. I quickly learned that if I began to consciously think about the meaning or significance of the lyrics while I was writing them then the finished song would inevitably sound contrived. On most occasions I didn't realize what a song was about until I was composing the third or fourth verse. The best songs I've written are those that came together musically and lyrically in less than twenty minutes. In other words, as corny as it sounds, they just flowed out of me.

For the first time in my life I was tapping into my innermost thoughts and feelings. I was tapping into my subconscious being. And what I discovered surprised me. I had felt a seemingly inexplicable angst for years, but now I could identify what that angst consisted of, even if I didn't always understand its roots. Through songwriting I began to feel empowered in a whole new way. Songwriting allowed me to begin understanding myself and, by extension, to begin determining if I actually liked myself. The short answer to that question was that I didn't like myself. This realization gave me a sense of agency in my life that I'd never before experienced. Previously, I'd always been reacting to the world around me, but now I realized that my meandering life path had not been motivated so much by self-discovery as by self-avoidance. This awakening began to lead me down a much healthier and more enlightened path than the one I'd been travelling on for years.

By 1988, my evolving philosophical and political views meant that my situation at work was becoming untenable. I could no longer tolerate the rampant racist, sexist and homophobic remarks of my co-workers and bosses. I also began speaking out against the relatively low pay we received compared to that earned by workers at nearby unionized supermarkets. Not surprisingly, the owners began viewing me as an irritant. I was also finding it increasingly difficult to continue subjecting myself to the conservative attitudes that dominated suburban Detroit in general.

At the same time, my personal growth and my passion for music meant that Elizabeth found herself married to a very different person than the one she'd met four years earlier. I finally admitted to myself that both my marriage and my attempt to live a "normal" life were farces. In reality, I'd married an idea, a lifestyle concept, not a person. And so I left Elizabeth and filed for divorce. She was not impressed with my unilateral decision about our future. After all, she'd grown up believing in the fairy-tale dream of two people falling in love, getting married and living happily ever after, or at least until death do us part. Therefore, even though she wasn't happy in our marriage, she was unwilling to relinquish that dream.

And so began an ugly divorce battle during which her primary objective appeared to be to make me suffer as much as possible and, I feared, to hold out "until death do us part." Eventually, after one-and-a-half years of wrangling over what should have been a straight-forward settlement, Elizabeth and I signed the papers. I imagined that she'd finally reached a point where making her own life miserable just to make mine miserable was no longer worth it. Whatever the reason, I was finally free and, having realized that I was destined to live a more unconventional life, I quit my job as a butcher and prepared to move to New York City.

I had recently visited New York for the first time to attend Steve's wedding, in which he married an Italian-American woman named Gigi. Steve had a loft apartment in the Tribeca neighborhood of Lower Manhattan and was focused on his artwork. When I visited him I fell in love with New York City. New York represented everything that suburban Detroit wasn't. It was vibrant, stimulating, multicultural and contained a large artistic community. I knew that New York was where I had to go to focus on my music. But before I made the move there, I decided to take the opportunity afforded me by this moment of transition to further explore my growing fascination with Latin America. This time, however, the trip wouldn't be motivated by a subconscious desire to run away from myself, but by a genuine desire to learn more about that amazing part of the world.

CHAPTER 5

Welcome to the Jungle

Following my divorce in the fall of 1989 I flew from Detroit to Costa Rica and then travelled to Ecuador. My ultimate objective was to visit the Amazon Rainforest, a part of Latin America I'd been longing to experience for years. But to get to Ecuador from Costa Rica, I had to pass through Panama and Colombia.

The situation was tense when I arrived in Panama City because the game of political one-upmanship between the US government and Panamanian leader Manuel Noriega was reaching its zenith. For much of the 1980s Noriega had been a CIA asset who was involved in cocaine trafficking, something that the Reagan administration had been willing to overlook while it needed the Panamanian strongman to support the US-backed Contras in their attempt to overthrow Nicaragua's Sandinista government. But by the end of the decade, Noriega was exhibiting signs of independence and the winding down of the Contra War had made him dispensable.

I never imagined when I left Panama that less than a month later the Bush administration would invade the country, overthrow Noriega and ship him to Florida to face drug trafficking charges. The human cost of catching a single drug trafficker was immense, with as many as four thousand Panamanians killed during the bombing and invasion. The Panama invasion marked the first time that the war on drugs was used to justify direct US military intervention in a Latin American nation. The threat of communism had collapsed along with the Berlin Wall, but Washington now had a new post-Cold War justification for militarily intervening in its "own backyard."

I left Panama and spent five days travelling through Colombia before crossing the border into Ecuador. My first few days in Ecuador were spent in the capital Quito where I explored the different possibilities for traveling to the Amazon region, which Ecuadorians call "El Oriente." I decided on the Napo River due to its accessibility and affordability. I flew in a rickety, old World War Two-era DC-3 from Quito, which sits over nine thousand feet up in the Andes, down to a small town on the Napo River officially called Francisco de Orellano but known locally as Coca. It was from this spot that the town's namesake, a Spanish conquistador, had set off to become the first European to cross the continent from the Andes Mountains to the Atlantic Ocean on the Amazon River. And while the Spanish conquistadors might be long gone, I would soon learn that a new conquest had recently occurred in that part of the Amazon. This time, instead of Spaniards wielding swords and cannons, the conquistadors were North American corporations that had come armed with oil drilling equipment.

For the most part, Coca was hot, humid, dusty and bustling with the energy of a frontier town. It wasn't a particularly pleasant place, and I wanted to escape down the Napo River as soon as possible. After futilely waiting three days for a supply boat that the dockworkers had told me daily would leave "mañana," I decided to find an alternative mode of transportation. I met an indigenous family that was willing to sell me a dugout canoe and paddle for the equivalent of fifteen dollars. I loaded my backpack into my new canoe and set off down the Napo. While the size of the Napo pales in comparison to the Amazon River, which it runs into several hundred miles downstream, it was still an impressive waterway.

The most prominent indigenous groups in the Napo region were the Huaorani, Cofán, Secoya and Quichua, all of whom had succeeded in remaining mostly isolated from the outside world until the middle of the 20th century. By the time I visited the region in 1989, many of those indigenous families living along the banks of the Napo had become accustomed to outsiders, although most outsiders were Latinos not gringos. Meanwhile, many clans still lived relatively isolated deeper in the rainforest.

I had no experience handling a canoe, which might lead many to think that paddling through the Amazon jungle under such circumstances would constitute a ludicrous, or even stupid, undertaking. And you know what? They'd be right. I paid the price for being a novice within hours of starting out on my journey. I was being carried along by a current that was particularly fast on one bend in the river. There was a large tree trunk protruding through the surface of the water and the current was rapidly carrying me directly towards it. I paddled frantically in an effort to avoid the tree, but only succeeded in turning my canoe sideways. I broadsided the tree and my canoe immediately capsized. I instinctively grabbed my backpack with one hand and the tree with the other and hung on for dear life. My canoe was nowhere to be seen, nor was there any sign of human habitation. I was all alone and surrounded by fast-flowing water and jungle. My backpack quickly became waterlogged and grew very heavy. The Napo River was a dark, muddy brown color that made it impossible to see even one inch below the surface. As I hung on to that tree trunk I found myself anticipating a creature taking a bite out of my legs beneath the surface of that murky water. The thought of piranha, electric eels, anacondas and crocodiles encircling me was nerve-wracking.

I hung on to the tree trunk for a while hoping that a passing boat would see me, but there was no sign of human life anywhere. I finally decided to try and swim across the current to the shore, which lay about sixty feet away. But as soon as I released the tree trunk I realized the futility of that idea. I made it about five feet towards the shore before the current had carried me fifty feet further downstream and directly towards a large expanse of branches and logs floating on the water's surface. The realization that the force of the current might drag me below the surface and under the floating lumber filled me momentarily with terror. Stubbornly holding onto my backpack with one hand, for God knows what reason, I used my other hand to grasp at branches. The first few broke or slipped out of my hand, but I eventually gained a hold. I dragged myself up onto a partly submerged log and, half-in and half-out the water, succeeded in pulling myself through the floating lumber to the shore. I heaved myself and my backpack out of the river and breathed a heavy sigh of relief.

Since I hadn't seen any dwellings for a while prior to capsizing, I decided to walk along the riverbank in the direction I'd been travelling. After about thirty minutes I stumbled upon a humble wooden hut on stilts. It was the home of an indigenous family and, after recovering from their initial surprise at finding a soaking wet gringo standing at their door, they invited me to sit down and listened to my story. The father then dispatched his two sons, aged eleven and eight, to recover my canoe.

I stayed with that family for three days, during which the two sons provided me with some much-needed canoe handling lessons. The boys also informed me that there had been little chance of me being attacked while in the river because most creatures preferred slow-moving water. They also told me that I should have continued paddling straight ahead when I saw the submerged tree and the canoe would have simply glanced off it. It was all very humbling. When it came time to leave and continue my journey down the Napo, the family loaded up my canoe with a sack of fresh papaya. I'm sure I left them scratching their heads and wondering how on earth the "white man" had managed to conquer so much of the world.

I spent almost two weeks on the Napo River. There were a few small villages and the occasional isolated single-family dwelling situated along the river, but I was mostly surrounded by uninhabited rainforest. I had never felt so beyond the laws of human society as when I was paddling through the Amazon in my dugout canoe. I felt entirely at the mercy of nature. I mused that living in harmony with nature seemed to be the only way a human being could survive there. Never before had I felt so insignificant.

One evening, I was sitting alone on the riverbank listening to the sounds of the rainforest and staring up at the stars, which were absolutely dazzling because I was so close to the equator and there were no electric lights for miles around. It was one of the most beautiful moments of solitude I had ever experienced. At the same time, I wanted nothing more than to have someone special there to share that moment with me. It made me realize that we humans, at our core, are social beings.

The indigenous people living along the Napo had retained much of their traditional way of life, but one of the three families that I stayed with was markedly different than the others. That particular family consisted of a father and daughter who had a melancholy and defeated air about them that were truly disturbing. They were the second stop on my river journey and I arrived at their village on the fifth day after my departure from Coca.

It was late afternoon when I stepped out of my canoe and tied it to a tree. I clambered up the riverbank with my backpack slung over my right shoulder and walked through an eerily deserted village. After a few minutes I came across a small girl sitting in the dirt in front of a wooden house on stilts. She was five-years-old with long black hair and was dressed in a yellow and white striped shirt and white shorts. She looked up at me and proudly displayed a small green parrot held captive in her hands. Momentarily, the father appeared in the doorway of the house. I introduced myself and inquired if there was somewhere I could spend the night and if I could purchase some food. He told me his name was Julio and then said, "You're welcome to sleep in the house next door. It's empty, but has a hammock."

There were fifteen or so abandoned houses along the riverbank and, apparently, another dozen houses situated beyond a grassy recreation area. According to Julio, most of those houses were also abandoned and only a handful of residents remained. Julio invited me back to his dwelling for something to eat. To my surprise he asked if I would like a Coca-Cola to drink with my meal of fish, rice and beans. His daughter Liliana ran over to a hut beside the house and when she opened the door I saw that it was stocked from floor to ceiling with crates of Coca-Cola. Naturally curious, I asked Julio how that virtually abandoned village in the middle of the Amazon Rainforest had come to be so fully-stocked with bottles of Coca-Cola.

"For fifteen years the oil company was here," Julio began. "They came and promised us jobs that would provide us a better life. And so we abandoned our traditional lifestyle of hunting, fishing and gathering forest crops. They said that we no longer needed to do those things because the company would provide us with all the food we needed in return for our labor. They made us believe that it would always be that way."

"What happened?" I inquired.

"The oil ran out and the company left a little more than a year ago," he answered, a touch of bitterness creeping into his voice.

"And what happened to all the villagers?"

"They also left. They went looking for work elsewhere. Some are in Coca, some in Lago Agrio, and some in Quito," he explained. "It was difficult to return to our old way of life because the animals were gone and the oil had polluted the forest and the streams. Also, many of the younger ones had no interest in learning the old ways after experiencing the things that the company had provided like alcohol, Coca-Cola, canned food, electricity and many other things that we had never seen before. My wife was one of those who left. She went to Quito because she didn't like it here anymore."

I sat there stunned. While I had anticipated learning many fascinating things during my trip to the Amazon, I'd never imagined witnessing such devastation as had been wrought upon that indigenous village.

"So all this Coca-Cola is left from when the company was here?" I asked.

"Yes," he replied. "My job was to run the store that sold Coca-Cola and other things that the company brought in on its boats. Now all I have left is the Coca-Cola."

When I awoke the next morning I decided to explore the village. I wandered across the recreation field and past the abandoned buildings that lined one side of it. At the other end of the field was another collection of dwellings similar to those on the riverbank. All but two of the houses were empty. Three indigenous men and two women were the sole remaining residents in that section of the village. It was about nine o'clock in the morning when I came across the three men, all of whom appeared to be in their fifties, sitting in front of one of the houses. They greeted me and invited me to join them for a drink. I sat with them but declined the drink they offered, which was some form of moonshine. I quickly realized that they'd either been drinking all night or had started very early that morning, since their words were slurred and they were unsteady on their feet. The women, meanwhile, appeared to be busying themselves with chores inside the house.

The conversation began pleasantly enough as we discussed my journey down the river, but then things began to turn ugly. The drunkest of the three men stood up, grabbed his machete and launched into a rant against US oil companies.

"Those sons of bitches have ruined us. They came here and ruined our land, our water and our community. If there were an American here right now, I'd cut his head off," he raged, while swirling his machete around recklessly.

Luckily, I'd told them that I was British and hadn't informed them that I lived in the United States. While the other two men tried to calm down the inebriated machete wielder, I began to excuse myself. But the angry drunk would have none of it. He had a new target upon which to vent his anger and resentment, and he was not about to let me slip away. Grabbing the front of my shirt and waving the machete a little too close to my head for comfort, my embittered host continued with his anti-American rant. I again tried to take my leave before he decided that a British head would suffice in the absence of an American one.

Finally, his friends got him back into his chair and I quickly bid them farewell and made my escape. Not wanting to appear panicked, I walked as fast as I could without breaking into a run. As I made my way towards the recreation field I repeatedly glanced over my shoulder to ensure that I was not being followed. I spent the rest of the day on the riverbank hoping that the three drunken men would not decide to venture over to that side of the village—and they didn't.

The next morning I said goodbye to Julio and Liliana and resumed my journey down the Napo River. Alone in my canoe, I struggled to come to terms with the devastation visited on that small indigenous community; first by the arrival of the oil company, and then by its departure. I was also struck by the similarities between the way that corporate capitalism had impacted the lives of those indigenous people and my father.

By the time I left the Amazon and returned to the United States I felt an intimate bond with Latin America and its people. The introspection that I was engaged in during that period allowed me to recognize that some of the most significant and transformative experiences in my life had occurred in Latin America. As a result, what began as a curiosity about the region following my discharge from the

Marines had evolved into a passion. I realized that Latin America would continue to play an important role in my life. Although in what way, I didn't yet know.

CHAPTER 6

My Political Awakening

During the 1990s I continued my process of self-reflection as I sought to make sense of my many personal experiences and the things that I had witnessed over the years. During that decade I lived in New York City with the exception of three years spent in Las Vegas to attend the University of Nevada. Through both self-education and my formal university education I began to contextualize many of my life experiences, particularly those in Latin America. The result was a profound shift away from Ayn Rand and the myth of individualism toward a more compassionate view of people and society. At the heart of this shift was a deeper understanding of the role played by the US government and corporations in the injustices that are intrinsic to capitalism.

I supported myself in New York City by driving a cab four nights a week while spending most of my free time working on music and playing gigs in the city's club scene. Two years after arriving in New York I entered into my first really meaningful long-term relationship. I met Jacqui at a New Year's Eve party in 1992 in the Brooklyn apartment of a mutual friend. Jacqui was five-feet two inches tall, had long, straight, silky black hair, and Asian features inherited from her Korean mother. Her father was an Italian-American who owned a bakery on Long Island, where Jacqui grew up. Six months into our relationship, we found a small two-bedroom, rent-controlled apartment in the East Village and moved in together.

Jacqui proved to be one of the most influential people in my life and the degree of personal growth that I experienced during the decade we were together was quite astounding. While a growing conscious shift was already occurring regarding my personal philosophy and political views, it was Jacqui who helped me to more fully comprehend that people are both rational and emotional beings. She also made me acknowledge that I was seriously incapable of expressing my feelings. In short, she helped me realize that I was, in many ways, a macho jerk.

The process of getting in touch with my emotional side proved to be long and painful, not just for me, but for Jacqui too. Ultimately, it led me to begin seriously questioning many of the values linked to our Western culture, particularly the degree to which we have hyper-valued the human capacity for rational behavior. Males in particular have been socialized to believe that expressions of feelings and displays of emotion are signs of weakness. In our male-dominated society such traits are identified with the "weaker" female sex, while purely rational and logical behaviors are considered to be both superior and primarily male qualities. For women to appear strong and independent, we're often led to believe that they need to exhibit these so-called male traits. This reality was exemplified by the lead female characters in Ayn Rand's novels and by many "successful" female political leaders such as former British Prime Minister Margaret Thatcher, appropriately nicknamed the "Iron Lady."

I had functioned almost exclusively as a rational being, viewing rational behavior and logical thinking as the apex of human existence. Meanwhile, my emotional side was not only repressed, it was buried way down deep in some dark hole. In truth, I was terrified of it. But the minute I began to understand that both our rational and emotional responses to life are legitimate and essential, it was no longer possible to accept the rational-based philosophy of Ayn Rand and others of her ilk, including many Enlightenment thinkers. Human beings are both rational and emotional animals—after all, it's what makes us human, and fallible. But too many of us males view our emotional side as a weakness to be ashamed of and shunned rather than as a natural human response to the reality of living in an unpredictable world.

My evolving personal philosophical views inevitably had repercussions for my political views. It had finally become evident to me that the extreme individual responsibility advocated by Ayn Rand had little relation to the reality experienced by billions of people around the world. For some there may be an element of truth to the so-called American Dream, in which all one has to do is work hard to get ahead—particularly if one is white, male and educated—but in reality it represents the impossible dream for a majority of the world's population. My previous experiences helped me to understand that working hard and "doing the right thing" were no guarantors of anything, particularly for millions of the world's poor. I'd met countless Latin Americans who worked harder and longer hours than me and most Americans I knew, and yet they had little hope of ever escaping the poverty and oppression that they endured daily. Their brutal reality was not due to any failing of their own; it was directly linked to the system under which they lived—and that system was capitalism.

Meanwhile, I was feeling burned out on New York's music scene; not on the music itself, but rather on the daily promotional grind and the assembly line attitude of the business side of the club scene. So Jacqui and I decided to sublet our apartment and take a break from it all. We had gotten married in Las Vegas on New Year's Day in 1996 while on a trip there to visit her mother and sister. Nine months later we decided to pack up our bags, climb onto our Honda 750cc motorbike and head out on a six-week road trip that would ultimately return us to Sin City.

The plan was to take a one-year motorcycle trip with no final destination in mind and then return to New York to resume playing music. We headed out of the city in September 1996 unaware that we wouldn't return home for three years. We rode down the length of the Appalachian Mountains, visited New Orleans and Louisiana bayou country, travelled across Texas and camped in the Guadalupe Mountains National Park before spending several days at a hostel in Truth or Consequences, New Mexico. We then decided to head down into Arizona and on into Mexico where we spent a week hiking and relaxing in Copper Canyon before making our way over to the Pacific Coast for a few days on the beach. We'd been on the road for six weeks at that point and were running low on money, so we decided to head north to Las Vegas to visit Jacqui's family and to replenish our funds before resuming the trip.

Upon arriving in Las Vegas we re-evaluated our plans. Our brief visit to Mexico had rekindled my passion for Latin America. And, after six weeks of freedom on the road, the thought of eventually returning to the rat race of

New York's music scene and doing uninspiring jobs to help support us did not appeal to me. So Jacqui and I decided that we would stay in Las Vegas for as long as it took me to finish my degree in Political Science at the University of Nevada, Las Vegas (UNLV). Jacqui felt that staying in Las Vegas would also provide her with the opportunity to spend quality time with her mother and sister.

I got a job as a security guard at a construction site while attending blackjack dealing school. My plan was to get a job in a casino in order to pay my way through university. A small sign in the office of the security company that I worked for caught my attention when I went to pick-up my first paycheck. The sign informed employees that the company was going to begin making health insurance available. The cost to the employee would be $450 a month. Meanwhile, I was earning $6.00 an hour, which came to a gross income of $240 a week. So, in theory, my fellow employees and I had access to health care coverage. In reality, we couldn't afford to spend almost half of our monthly wages on health care premiums and still have enough left over to cover income taxes, rent, utilities, groceries, gas and other incidentals. Needless to say, few employees enrolled in the health care plan, instead remaining among the tens of millions of workers in the United States who lacked health coverage.

I hadn't had health insurance since leaving my butcher's job in suburban Detroit seven years earlier. I couldn't afford to purchase health coverage as a taxi driver in New York, and would often cure the sinusitis I came down with annually by illegally buying black market antibiotics from corner stores in a Dominican neighborhood. Rumor had it that they were horse antibiotics smuggled in from the Dominican Republic. All I knew was that they could be purchased without a doctor's prescription, were affordable and worked. Despite my lack of medical insurance for much of my adult life, I had never seriously questioned the structure of the US health care system.

The private for-profit US health care system makes each person primarily responsible for obtaining their own health care coverage, whether through their employment or independently, which correlates perfectly with the philosophy of Ayn Rand. After all, didn't national health care constitute socialism? The increasing costs of health care and the desire to maximize profits led employers to begin demanding that employees cover a portion or all of the monthly premiums. This shift has proved particularly problematic for workers in the low-paid, non-unionized service sector, because many do not have sufficient disposable income to contribute to their health insurance premiums. This was the reality I was faced with in my new job as a security guard.

Standing in that office I suddenly realized the ludicrousness of a system in which access to health care is primarily linked to an individual's employment rather than being a right for all citizens. It is perhaps the ultimate illustration of a government abdicating its social responsibility. After all, tens of millions of people work as security guards, taxi drivers, store clerks, delivery people and in scores of other professions that do not provide them with access to affordable health care. These workers earn too much money to qualify for Medicaid and not enough to purchase insurance individually or through their workplace, that's if their workplace even offers a medical plan. In short, it is the working poor who lack access to affordable health care. The same lack of access to health care applies to spouses of the working poor who stay home to raise children and to musicians and other artists who struggle to survive financially. And yet all of these people play crucial roles in maintaining a functioning and vibrant society.

The structure of the US health care system didn't make sense to me from a humanitarian point of view. The fact that almost fifty million people in the United States lack adequate health care coverage because they work in the "wrong" field constitutes a gross injustice. The private for-profit health industry in the United States lies at the heart of the issue. And a fundamental problem with the private system is that an individual's health care is often determined by an insurance company representative rather than by a doctor and, being a corporation, the insurance company's primary objective is profit not health.

Health care in the United States has long been considered a business rather than a social right. And the number of Americans without health insurance has increased since the Reagan years as growing numbers of the workforce have been shifted out of well-paid, unionized jobs with benefits into low-paid, non-unionized service sector work that does not offer affordable health care plans. And while capitalism is supposedly about efficiency, the US health care system is the most inefficient when compared with other wealthy nations that have national health care programs because it has the smallest percentage of the money spent in the health sector actually going to health care. But efficiency in the US health care system is not about the delivery of health care, it's about facilitating profit generation for corporations operating in the health industry.

My growing political awareness was creating a desire to achieve an even greater understanding of the system under which I lived. To fulfil that desire I became an avid reader of books about US politics and Latin America, particularly US policy in Latin America. An instrumental figure whose writings contributed to my growing understanding of Washington's role in the world was Noam Chomsky who, while considered by many around the world to be the leading critic of US foreign policy, has remained largely unknown to the average American. I also took courses at UNLV taught by Professor Thomas Wright that examined the politics and history of Latin America, as well as the US role in the region. Tom became a good friend who, in conjunction with my self-education, helped me to more comprehensively contextualize my own personal experiences in Latin America and to better understand some of the power structures at play in the United States and throughout the world.

The globalized economic model we live under today began to fully emerge during the 1980s as a result of President Reagan's economic policies, which were known domestically as "supply-side economics" or "Reaganomics." They represented a significant shift from the Keynesian protectionist model that had emerged following the Great Depression and that had established a social safety net in the form of unemployment insurance, public housing, welfare payments and other aspects of the so-called welfare state. It was during those decades that the populations of the United States, Canada and Western European nations became predominantly middle class. But under Reagan, the US government began downsizing many of those social programs and prioritizing the needs of the private sector over the public sector

Reagan's policies were heavily influenced by the theories of an economist at the University of Chicago named Milton Friedman, who became an economic advisor to the president. Friedman's theories, which have been labelled "neoliberalism" by some, advocate a free-market economic model in which the private sector dominates almost every sphere of life and the government's primary role is to protect the interests of that private sector. The term neoliberalism reflects the 19th century economic use of the word "liberal" rather than the 20th century political meaning. In economic terms, liberal means free from government intervention, referring to the free-market economy that largely existed in Britain during the mid-1800s. Hence, neoliberal means the "new" liberal era, or a return to the days of small government with little regulation of the private sector.

Neoliberals argue that the private sector could run the economy more efficiently than governments and in a free trade environment would achieve greater economic growth. Under such conditions, capitalist entrepreneurs and corporations would re-invest the wealth generated by economic growth in order to generate even more growth and the benefits would "trickle-down" to all sectors of society in the form of job creation.

During the 1980s, President Reagan in the United States, Prime Minister Margaret Thatcher in Britain and Prime Minister Brian Mulroney in Canada all oversaw the entrenchment of neoliberalism in their respective countries. At the time, the policies and rhetoric of Reagan had seemed logical to me, even appearing to be common sense. After all, much of Ayn Rand's libertarian philosophy fit nicely with the conservative vision of the American Dream. It reflected many of the ideals, including free market capitalism, espoused by Reagan. Joseph Stiglitz, a Nobel laureate and the chief economist for the World Bank during the 1990s, alluded to Rand's influence on Reagan when he noted that the president appointed Alan Greenspan as chairman of the Federal Reserve Board in 1987 because he wanted someone who believed in de-regulating the financial sector and "he found in him a devotee of the objectivist philosopher and free-market zealot Ayn Rand."

During Reagan's eight years in office, the rights of workers and unions were diminished and social spending was drastically cut. As early as 1981, Reagan made clear his anti-union attitude when he fired more than eleven thousand striking air traffic controllers who had ignored his order to return to work. Reagan's anti-union policies would contribute to a major decline in union membership in the United States from a peak of 21 million workers in 1979 to 15 million by 2003.

The process of privatization, particularly at the state and municipal levels, also contributed to the decline in union membership. Throughout the 1980s and 1990s, responsibility for garbage disposal, water management, utilities, public housing and even the operation of prisons was turned over to companies in the private sector. As a result, well-paid, unionized, public sector jobs with decent benefits were replaced with lower-paid, non-unionized, private sector employment that offered few, if any, benefits. At the same time, cutbacks in social spending made the poor and unemployed more vulnerable during economic downturns. Public spending cuts by the Reagan administration also resulted in thousands of mentally ill people being evicted from state facilities, contributing to the explosion in the country's homeless population. I witnessed the consequences of those callous social policies in New York when it became clear to me that most of the homeless people living on the streets of the city were suffering from serious psychological problems and drug addictions that required medical treatment. But according to Reagan, as he stated in 1984, the homeless are "homeless, you might say, by choice."

Meanwhile, the Reagan administration's neoliberal policies benefitted wealthy Americans, particularly corporate executives and investment bankers. The dog-eat-dog world of corporate takeovers began to intensify during the Reagan years. Corporate executives and major investors in financial centers like New York City represented the successful face of the neoliberal model as they earned massive fortunes from mergers and market speculation that left millions of Americans awash in economic insecurity. The value of the mergers and acquisitions that took place in 1980 amounted to $50 billion; fifteen years later they totaled $450 billion. Those takeovers proved hugely profitable for corporate executives, major shareholders and the financial investors involved in orchestrating the deals.

Reaganomics initiated a dramatic increase in the incomes of the CEOs of America's largest corporations when compared to the earnings of their employees, thereby increasing inequality in the country. In 1980, CEO's earned 42 times the salary of their average worker. That income gap would increase dramatically over the ensuing three decades as the CEOs of the country's largest five hundred corporations would pocket 343 times more than their average employee by 2010. In the neoliberal era, the filthy rich of the business world began achieving celebrity status as the worshipping of the almighty dollar filtered down throughout an increasingly consumerist society.

The deregulation of the financial sector that began during the Reagan era not only led to an increase in corporate takeovers and eventually the financial crisis of 2008, it also resulted in some Wall Street investment bankers enriching themselves through illegal activities such as insider trading and Ponzi schemes. By the mid-1980s, Ivan Boesky had amassed a fortune of more than $200 million, much of it from illegal investments based on tips from corporate contacts. He ended up serving only two years in prison. At the same time, Michael Milken was earning billions of dollars through his involvement in funding corporate takeovers and other investment activities. In 1989, Milken was indicted on ninety-eight counts of racketeering and fraud that included insider trading. He ultimately entered into a plea bargain under which he pled guilty to only six of the counts and served less than two years behind bars.

And while Wall Street investors were pocketing hundreds of millions of dollars orchestrating and investing in corporate takeovers, the huge debts assumed to finance the deals were repaid by downsizing, selling off or closing the least profitable parts of a newly-acquired company. As a result, thousands of workers would suddenly find themselves unemployed or forced to take significant pay cuts in order to cover the costs of simply transferring a profitable company from one billionaire owner to another billionaire owner.

Driving a cab in New York exposed me to both extremes of neoliberal America. I regularly ferried wealthy financial investors from their Park Avenue penthouse apartments to their Wall Street offices and expensive restaurants. Meanwhile, on the way, we would often pass homeless people begging on the streets and desperately trying to protect themselves from the elements in their cardboard box abodes.

The government of President George H. W. Bush continued down the same neoliberal path as the Reagan administration. The arrival of Democrat Bill Clinton in the White House in 1993 did little to alter the direction of the country or its promotion of neoliberalism both at home and abroad. The Republican and Democratic parties have proven to be equally pro-neoliberal. In fact, economic policymaking is one area that has been thoroughly bipartisan since the introduction of Reaganomics in the early 1980s. The same can be said for the Conservative and Labour parties in Britain and the Conservatives and Liberals in Canada.

The era of neoliberal globalization wasn't actually initiated by Reagan, it began on the original 9/11, by which I mean September 11, 1973. On that day a US-backed military coup overthrew the democratically-elected socialist government of Chile, which resulted in the death of President Salvador Allende. Chile had been attempting to show the world that a peaceful democratic transition to socialism was possible, but even that was unacceptable to the United States. Washington's imperialist arrogance was exemplified by US Secretary of State Henry Kissinger, who said at the time, "I don't see why we need to stand by and watch a country go communist due to the irresponsibility of its people. The issues are much too important for the Chilean voters to be left to decide for themselves."

Those Chilean voters suddenly found themselves governed by a military dictatorship headed by the army's General Augusto Pinochet. The new regime had two primary objectives. The first was to capture, incarcerate, torture, kill and exile as many leftists and critics of the coup regime as possible—as quickly as possible. The second objective was to replace the socialist policies implemented by the Allende government with free market capitalism. The Chilean dictator was able to effectively carry out his initial objective because he had control over the country's military and intelligence apparatus. In the first few years following the coup it is estimated that three thousand Chileans were killed or "disappeared" by the regime, tens of thousands were imprisoned and tortured, and almost half a million fled into exile. In order to achieve his second objective, Pinochet turned to a group of Chilean economists that had studied under Milton Friedman at the University of Chicago. This group of Chileans became known as "The Chicago Boys."

The Pinochet government, with US backing, turned Chile into the testing ground for Friedman's theories and, two years after the coup, Friedman himself visited Chile and met with Pinochet. During his visit, Friedman never once criticized the dictatorship for its extensive human rights abuses, which had for the most part eliminated all opposition to the government's plan to turn Chile into a neoliberal paradise. But at the time of Friedman's visit Chile was far from a paradise, and not only because of the dire human rights situation. The nation's wealth was not trickling down to the majority of the population. In fact, the economy was rapidly deteriorating under the neoliberal model and the country was experiencing a severe social crisis with Chileans enduring high unemployment and hyperinflation. During the first two years of neoliberalism, unemployment soared from 4 percent to 25 percent and real wages fell to a third of their value only five years earlier. Chileans didn't suffer this "shock therapy" for only a few months as Friedman had initially predicted, they suffered it for years as unemployment soared even though more than half a million Chileans had fled the country. And then, in 1976, while millions of Chileans were still enduring the "shock," Friedman received the Nobel Memorial Prize for Economics.

Following its success in Chile, US foreign policy became rooted in the promotion of neoliberalism globally. While the United States also took a militaristic approach to implementing neoliberalism in El Salvador, Nicaragua and numerous other countries, it utilized an alternative strategy to achieve its objectives throughout most of the global South (Latin America, Africa and Asia). During the middle decades of the 20th century, the US government had encouraged private banks, as well as US-dominated international financial institutions such as the International Monetary Fund (IMF) and the World Bank, to provide loans to dictatorships and quasi-democratic regimes in pro-capitalist nations throughout the global South, or the Third World as it was commonly known at the time. While some of the money benefited local populations, much of it flowed into the pockets of the corrupt political and economic elites who ensured that their nations remained staunchly anti-communist during the Cold War. Ultimately, irresponsible lending by Western banks and irresponsible borrowing by non-democratic regimes allied with the United States resulted in many countries becoming mired in a severe debt crisis by the early 1980s.

Many nations in the global South that were struggling to service their foreign debts had little choice but to turn to the IMF for bailout loans. The IMF, which over the previous decade had become staffed primarily with Milton Friedman's disciples, used the debt crisis as a conduit for dismantling the Keynesian protectionist model and replacing it with neoliberalism. The IMF placed conditions on its loans that required borrowing nations to implement neoliberal-inspired Structural Adjustment Programs (SAPs), also known as austerity measures. Under these austerity measures, state-owned companies were privatized while trade and investment barriers were eliminated in order to attract foreign investment and spur economic growth. Similarly, the World Bank began placing conditions on its development loans that also required the implementation of neoliberal reforms. This policy approach by both the IMF and the World Bank became known as the "Washington Consensus" because both institutions were based in Washington, DC and were closely aligned ideologically with the United States. In fact, the United States held veto power over any loan decisions made by either institution.

Multinational corporations took advantage of the new favorable investment conditions created by the IMF and World Bank by purchasing newly-privatized entities and exploiting cheap labor and natural resources throughout the global South. The deregulation that occurred under neoliberalism also weakened protections for workers and the environment, which were seen as barriers to free trade. In addition to establishing a favorable investment climate for multinational corporations, the IMF and World Bank loan conditions forced poor nations to produce for export instead of for domestic consumption so they could obtain sufficient dollars to service their foreign debts. As Joseph Stiglitz, Nobel Laureate and former chief economist at the World Bank, noted, "The mandate [of the IMF] often appears to be that of a bill collector for lending nations: its objective is to make sure that the debtor country has as large a war chest as possible to repay outstanding loans."

By the end of the 1980s, thanks in large part to the Reagan administration's foreign policies and the role of US-dominated international financial institutions such as the IMF and the World Bank, neoliberalism was being put into practice throughout most of Latin America. The social consequences proved devastating for hundreds of millions of people as inequality and poverty increased dramatically. The percentage of Latin Americans living in poverty had declined from 51 percent to 33 percent between 1960 and 1980, the last two decades of the Keynesian era when economic policymaking was more nationally focused, but had reached close to 50 percent again by the end of the first decade of neoliberal globalization.

This new and more comprehensive understanding of neoliberalism allowed me to better contextualize my personal experiences in Latin America. While I had already gained some understanding about the dire human rights situation in the Salvadoran Civil War, I learned from my research the degree to which the United States was complicit in that violence. Despite US-trained Salvadoran soldiers being responsible for the assassination of Archbishop Romero, the execution of four US churchwomen, the massacre of more than 900 civilians in the hamlet of El Mozote, the execution of four foreign journalists, and many other atrocities, President Reagan repeatedly certified that El Salvador had complied with the human rights conditions required for receiving US military aid.

Ultimately, the US government provided more than four billion dollars in military and economic aid to El Salvador during the 1980s, funding the largest US-supported military operation since Vietnam, and with a similar objective of quashing "communism." The Salvadoran army used that military aid to slaughter the very population it was supposed to be defending. I realized that it was not so much a war against communism as a war against peasants who sought to escape the repression and poverty they were enduring under a brutal and corrupt US-backed regime. By the end of the twelve-year war, more than seventy thousand Salvadoran civilians had been killed.

US military aid successfully prevented a guerrilla victory in El Salvador and, following the signing of peace accords in 1992, the US-backed government implemented neoliberal reforms that opened up that country's newly-established *maquiladoras*, or assembly plants, to US clothing manufacturers such as The Gap, Liz Claiborne and JC Penney. The vast pool of unemployed Salvadorans ensured that wages remained low while IMF-imposed neoliberal austerity measures forced the government to cut back social spending in a time of social crisis. The result was a mass exodus of Salvadorans seeking to escape unemployment and poverty. Most of those economic refugees flooded into the United States in search of jobs. By the end of the 20th century, the 2.5 million Salvadorans that lived in the United States amounted to more than one third of the population of El Salvador.

I was not only learning how to better contextualize my personal experiences in Latin America, but I was also beginning to understand the linkages between our comfortable lifestyles in wealthy nations of the global North—primarily North America and Europe—and the misery endured by so many in Latin America and other regions of the global South. The foreign policies, both military and economic, of powerful nations like the United States have sought to ensure the continuance of such global inequality. After all, "our" comfortable consumer lifestyles are dependent on us having access to "their" natural resources and cheap labor.

When people in the global South attempt to resist the exploitation of their labor and natural resources, the US government quickly labels them as subversives, or communists, or terrorists, or whatever moniker works at any given moment to justify repressing such behavior. This is precisely what occurred when people in Chile, El Salvador and Nicaragua began demanding democracy and freedom during the 1970s and 1980s; they were immediately labeled as anti-democratic and communist, and definitely as anti-American.

Arguably, the most visible expression of neoliberal globalization for Americans has been the North American Free Trade Agreement (NAFTA), which was signed by the governments of the United States, Canada and Mexico. The intent of NAFTA, which came into effect on January 1, 1994, was to create a free market for many agricultural and manufactured goods that transcended the borders of the three participating nations. The trade agreement dramatically reduced the amounts of tariffs that a government could apply to imports from a NAFTA partner, thereby facilitating the free movement of goods across borders. However, even though labor is considered a commodity under capitalism, workers did not have the same rights to move freely across borders as that possessed by capital and goods. Consequently, it proved much cheaper and more profitable for US and Canadian manufacturing companies to establish assembly plants in Mexico where they could pay workers a fraction of the amount they had previously paid their American and Canadian employees.

Meanwhile, NAFTA permitted the three countries to continue providing subsidies to their domestic agricultural producers, largely at the insistence of the US government. In reality, however, the United States and Canada could provide subsidies, but Mexico could not. The reason for the discrepancy rests in the broader neoliberal framework of global capitalism. Conditions placed on loans provided to Mexico by the IMF required that the Mexican government reduce its subsidies to the agricultural sector. So while NAFTA permitted Mexico to subsidize its agricultural sector, neoliberal austerity measures imposed on the country through IMF loan agreements ensured that Mexico could not subsidize its agricultural sector to the same degree as the United States and Canada.

This biased structure in favor of agri-businesses based in the United States and Canada has devastated the lives of millions of Mexican small farmers. NAFTA has resulted in the dumping of heavily-subsidized food products by US agri-businesses onto the Mexican market, the most devastating of which has been corn, the primary food staple in Mexico. Between 1997 and 2005, US agricultural subsidies to domestic corn producers averaged $4.5 billion a year. This allowed US agri-businesses to export corn to Mexico and to sell it for less than what it would have cost to produce if production were not subsidized. Not surprisingly, unsubsidized Mexican farmers could not compete with the cheap US corn, and imports from the United States quickly dominated the Mexican market.

Those Mexican farmers who could no longer compete with the subsidized US imports would, in theory, abandon agriculture and become wage laborers in Mexico's manufacturing sector and begin purchasing imported food. And Mexican farmers did abandon their lands; in fact, they abandoned them in startling numbers. By 2006, it was estimated that as many as two million Mexican farmers had quit farming. Many of Mexico's displaced peasants joined the exodus of poor people from various parts of the country to cities in northern Mexico that were experiencing a boom in the manufacturing sector during the early years of the trade agreement.

By 2000, NAFTA had created 700,000 manufacturing jobs in *maquiladoras*, or assembly plants, and the massive displacement of peasants from the countryside to the cities ensured a sufficient army of surplus labor to keep wages low, at an average of $1.74 an hour. But by 2003, more than 300,000 of those jobs had moved overseas, primarily to China, where the interests of multinational corporations were being better served through labor costs that were even lower than in Mexico. Therefore, even at its height, NAFTA failed to create enough new manufacturing jobs to accommodate the displaced peasant population. Furthermore, the social breakdown in Mexico and the massive flow of goods across the border that have occurred under NAFTA have made the country the center of the region's drug trafficking operations; a process that has been accompanied by rampant violence.

Given the devastating economic impacts of NAFTA, it is no surprise that the emergence of the so-called illegal immigration problem in the United States coincided with the implementation of the trade agreement. NAFTA's massive displacement of peasants and its failure to provide them with viable economic alternatives forced millions of people to seek their economic survival elsewhere, and the most logical destination for many has been the United States. Throughout much of the 20th century, the migration of Mexicans to the United States constituted little more than a trickle. As a result, there were only 4.8 million Mexican-born residents in the United States in 1994, the year that NAFTA went into effect. By 2000, that number had almost doubled to nine million, and it continued to grow after that.

NAFTA has also had negative consequences for Americans. The decline of Detroit is largely a consequence of NAFTA, and neoliberalism in general. Under NAFTA, the Big Three automobile companies closed factories in Detroit and shifted production to Mexico in order to save on labor costs. NAFTA was implemented on the heels of neoliberal policies that had already opened the US market to increasing numbers of imported cars. This one-two punch of increased imports followed by the shifting of domestic production to Mexico proved devastating for US auto workers. As a result, Detroit's population declined by more than half, from almost two million people in the 1970s to a mere 714,000 by 2012. The city has become the most recognizable and tragic example of de-industrialization in the United States in the neoliberal era.

By the late 1990s I was becoming increasingly aware that the logic behind the capitalist system had little to do with free market principles and everything to do with maximizing profits. For instance, I don't recall a single Wall Street investment banker standing up during the economic crisis of 2008 and declaring, "No, we don't want the government's bailout money because it violates our belief in the free market." Government policies that violate the free market doctrine such as bail-outs and subsidies that benefit corporations are perfectly acceptable under neoliberalism, while state funding of social programs to benefit the general population is portrayed as fiscally irresponsible. Ultimately, there is no contradiction in neoliberalism, it is doing precisely what it is intended to do: serve the interests of the world's largest corporations.

CHAPTER 7

From Gandhi to Che

I was an anomaly at UNLV for two reasons. Firstly, I was a mature student in my late thirties. Secondly, my political views were becoming increasingly progressive in a university where right-wing conservative attitudes dominated. To my amazement there were students in some of my political science courses who still believed at the end of the 20th century that only property owners should have the right to vote because property owners, according to their reasoning, were the only Americans who had a vested interest in the country. I decided to counter some of these right-wing views in 1998 by writing and publishing a one-page monthly newsletter that I distributed on campus. It was titled *Out of Left Field* and addressed a wide array of contemporary political issues. It also constituted my initial foray into the realm of political journalism.

I found it difficult to tolerate the conservative political attitudes that were so prominent in not only Las Vegas, but throughout much of that part of the country. Many people despised the federal government and complained about the "liberals" in Washington using taxpayers' hard-earned dollars to fund "un-American" activities such as the provision of social programs that support lazy, good-for-nothing, commie-loving bums in cities like New York. Meanwhile, the same people conveniently ignored the fact that Las Vegas and other cities in the southwest only exist because of massive federal government projects such as the Hoover Dam, which provides the water and electricity that makes it possible for people to live in the middle of the desert.

Many conservatives I met in the Southwest also seemed oblivious to the fact that residents of New York City paid far more in federal taxes each year than the city received back in funding from Washington. In contrast, most states in the Southwest, including Nevada, received more federal dollars than their residents paid in federal taxes. In fact, there was no sector of the US population that was more dependent on "big" government and federal subsidies than those who lived in the Southwest where conservative attitudes dominated.

I also found the culture of Las Vegas disturbing and grew to hate the fact that I was working as a blackjack and roulette dealer in an industry as socially destructive as casino gambling. My discomfort had nothing to do with religious or any other moral views of gambling, rather it related to the serious social problems connected to the industry. Las Vegas led the nation in suicides, bankruptcies and divorces. It also had the highest rates of family, and by extension child, homelessness.

Nevada did not collect state income tax from workers and because of this the state was viewed by residents as a shining example of small government. The state's revenues came primarily from the casinos. But the rampant social problems and the government's unwillingness to seriously address them illustrated the dire consequences that result from having a dominant private sector combined with a local government that has mostly abdicated its social responsibility to its citizens.

In many ways, the gambling industry in Las Vegas is a microcosm of capitalism. Las Vegas sells the dream that anybody can be successful and strike it rich, but in reality only a small minority ever does. The casino industry is controlled by corporations that not only earn huge profits from gambling, but also possess significant influence over the political leaders of both the city and the state. And behind the façade of glittering lights and wealth, there is a society drowning in social problems directly related to the economic model that Las Vegas depends on for its survival. As is the case with capitalism, money is God in Las Vegas, and human well-being is of little consequence to those who profit.

Ironically, only a decade earlier, many of the conservative attitudes I encountered in Las Vegas would have resonated with me. After all, I had previously been all about the supremacy of the culture of individualism. Consequently, I had believed that people's addictions and other problems resulted from their own weaknesses and were therefore solely their responsibility. By extension I had viewed state-sponsored social programs as misguided forms of compassion directed towards undeserving people. But I now understood that human beings are not islands unto themselves; they are individuals who exist in a variety of social contexts. Therefore, we are both individuals and social beings, and both of these two sides of us need to be acknowledged and accounted for.

Albert Einstein, whose scientific achievements are celebrated in the United States while the fact that he was a socialist is conveniently ignored in the teaching of US history and science, recognized this reality:

> Man is, at one and the same time, a solitary being and a social being. As a solitary being, he attempts to protect his own existence and that of those who are closest to him, to satisfy his personal desires, and to develop his innate abilities. As a social being, he seeks to gain the recognition and affection of his fellow human beings, to share in their pleasures, to comfort them in their sorrows, and to improve their conditions of life. ... It is evident, therefore, that the dependence of the individual upon society is a fact of nature which cannot be abolished.

Many people argue that the individualistic traits such as self-interest, competitiveness and greed that are so prominent in capitalist society are simply human nature. Therefore, any concept of a collective alternative is not really possible; it is utopian. But the prominence of these individualistic traits is a relatively recent occurrence in human history and a direct consequence of capitalism. It is the indoctrination process resulting from the education system, the media, elected officials, corporations and our workplace culture that has caused people to internalize these values and to view them as human nature. But nothing could be further from the truth. For if these individualistic values constitute human nature, then how do we explain thousands of years of human beings organizing themselves collectively in one form or another—and continuing to do so in many indigenous communities?

And we're not even that individualistic in our capitalist world. After all, most Americans drive virtually identical cars, live in virtually identical homes, and wear virtually identical clothes. In fact, is there any greater symbol of conformity and unanimity in our society than the suit and tie? We have bought into the idea of individualism while living our lives as virtual clones.

I realized that our prioritization of our individualistic side over our social side has become so dominant under capitalism that we had lost the ability to fulfill the social aspect of our being in any meaningful way. It seemed to me that we needed to begin correcting this imbalance between our individualistic side and our social side if we were to re-establish some sort of equilibrium and achieve a more just and sustainable society.

The questions I was asking about myself and the world in general, and my newfound comfort level with being an outsider, were all connected. Ever since my arrival in the United States at fifteen I had felt conflicted. On the one hand, I had maintained a rebellious streak, while on the other hand I'd sought to conform in order to gain recognition and acceptance. In many ways these two seemingly contradictory traits of my personality reflected the individual and social aspects of being human referred to by Einstein. The ultimate expression of my attempts to conform socially was my marriage to Elizabeth and the related failure of my attempt to live what I perceived to be a "normal" life in suburban Detroit. But when I began to question my individualistic philosophy, and by extension the culture of individualism that dominates in the United States, and to reflect on US policy in Latin America and the role of corporations in the lives of people everywhere, I began gaining a new sense of a social self that proved liberating. I was now connecting the dots between the different individualistic and social experiences in my life.

While enmeshed in the decadent culture of Las Vegas I also experienced a form of spiritual awakening that paralleled the intellectual enlightenment I was gaining through my self-education and at university. I had never been a spiritual person; in fact, I shunned any form of spiritualism the same way that I rejected organized religion. After all, I'd believed that the capacity to be rational and logical was the mark of a superior human being. I was baptized in the Church of England as a baby, but did not attend services during my childhood. My exposure to organized religion came in the English school system when we would attend assembly in the mornings and engage in prayer and hymn singing. It seemed to me that organized religion has traditionally been dominated by hierarchical institutions that seek to gain power over people. And while my views on organized religion remained unchanged over the years, something occurred in Las Vegas that led me to re-evaluate my attitude toward spirituality.

At the root of my spiritual awakening was a book by Mohandas Gandhi titled *The Story of My Experiments with Truth*. It was an autobiography of sorts in which the Indian independence leader detailed his personal struggle to be a good person, which could only be achieved through living an ethical life. Reading Gandhi led me to engage in even more intense self-reflection. It was through Gandhi that I began to contextualize philosophically many of my previous life experiences. While I had begun to question my Ayn Rand-influenced individualistic philosophy and my views of US foreign policy and corporate capitalism by my late twenties, I'd struggled to formulate a new philosophy of life. Gandhi's writings made me realize that I'd been shifting away from being an individual whose prominent character traits—conceit, cockiness, arrogance and competiveness—were little more than a façade established in part to protect a vulnerable teenager transplanted from one culture to another. Gandhi helped me to understand that my greatest internal conflict had consisted of my desire to be independent and individualistic while simultaneously yearning to be accepted by my peers and society in general. He also helped me to identify that my focus on music and its corresponding self-reflection illustrated that I'd already begun coming to terms with my inner conflicts.

Perhaps, most importantly, in addition to helping me understand my past, Gandhi provided me with valuable insights into the kind of person I wanted to be. And, surprisingly for me, he illuminated the degree to which I'd already moved in that direction, which is probably why the book resonated with me at that point in my life.

Ultimately, Gandhi led me to reflect on what it meant to be a "good person"—a moral and ethical human being. While being a "good person" is something we often think of as a fairly simple concept and an easily obtainable goal—for example, being nice and polite to people—I have come to discover that it's the most difficult thing in life. Even defining what it means to be a truly good person requires not only engaging in serious philosophical reflection, but also in painful self-evaluation. I realized that the way I interacted with other people reflected who I really was. Therefore, to be a good person meant I needed to exhibit those qualities that I believed constituted a moral and ethical human being. For me, being a good person was rooted in exhibiting honesty, integrity and compassion in my relations with others. Furthermore, it required faith to believe that I could both succeed in that personal quest and that it would ultimately have a positive impact on the world around me. In other words, as Gandhi noted, "Be the change that you want to see in the world." However, the motivation for being such a good person should not be the admiration and respect of others, but rather the attainment of an inner peace and contentment. I quickly learned that such a profound personal transformation was not going to occur overnight; it would require a lifetime commitment.

During this period I read another autobiography that was also hugely influential on me. It was titled *The Motorcycle Diaries: A Journey Around South America* and was written by Ernesto "Che" Guevara. In the book, the young Che documents his six-month odyssey travelling around South America in 1952. While he was already interested in political issues by the time he departed from his native Argentina, his experiences in Chile, Bolivia, Peru, Colombia and the Amazon would have a profound and radicalizing impact on him. It was those experiences that led him to become so passionate about, and concerned with, the plight of impoverished and oppressed peoples throughout Latin America. Within years of that journey he would fight alongside Fidel Castro in a guerrilla war that would eventually overthrow the US-backed dictatorship in Cuba and establish the first socialist government in the Western Hemisphere. Not surprisingly, given my own background in Latin America, Che's description of his early travel experiences and his resulting self-realization resonated with me. *The Motorcycle Diaries* led me to read many of Che's later, more overtly political, writings.

While Che has been reduced to a caricature of a violent Marxist revolutionary fighter in the eyes of North Americans, he is a symbol of much more than that to Cubans. Following victory in the revolutionary war, Che set about creating a new socialist society in Cuba with a fervor. He wrote about the need for a new consciousness rooted in compassion for our fellow human beings and the necessity of ensuring the well-being of all over defending the privilege of a few. On his days off from his government work he would toil alongside laborers in factories and on sugarcane plantations to promote a spirit of volunteerism, participation and solidarity. He was an avid reader who not only advocated free public education for all Cubans but also the importance of engaging in self-education and, more crucially, self-criticism. As a colleague of Che's during the early years of the revolution once told me, "Che was very demanding of everyone around him. But he was most demanding of himself." Ultimately, it was his compassion for others, particularly the poor and oppressed peoples of the world, that led Che to declare, "At the risk of seeming ridiculous, let me say that the true revolutionary is guided by a great feeling of love. It is impossible to think of a genuine revolutionary lacking this quality."

Both Gandhi and Che were revolutionaries who were killed because of their political beliefs. Both were passionate about combating social injustice, although they had very different approaches to realizing their objectives. Gandhi believed that injustice had to be fought non-violently. It was a moral issue for Gandhi because he believed that violence inevitably begets more violence. Therefore liberation, whether personal or social, gained through violence would only result in establishing a new violent person or society. On the other hand, if an individual adhered to the principles of non-violence then that person could never be defeated. That person could be imprisoned, beaten and even killed, but their faith and principles would remain intact. However, a failure to adhere to the principles of non-violence, and to instead resort to violence, would mean reducing one's self to the same moral level as one's oppressor. As Gandhi stated, "I am prepared to die, but there is no cause for which I am prepared to kill."

In contrast, Che firmly believed that in many instances liberation from violent oppression could not be achieved without resorting to violence. He believed that in many cases a violent revolution would be required to overthrow the ruling capitalist elites—whose power and wealth was dependent on the oppression of the majority of the world's population—because those in positions of power and wealth were not likely to peacefully relinquish their privilege. In Che's mind, taking up arms did not constitute the initiation of violence, rather it was an act of self-defense. After all, the oppression of millions of people required a system of violence to maintain their subservience. For Che, taking up arms against oppression also constituted a moral act, even a moral obligation.

While it might seem somewhat contradictory, both Gandhi and Che impacted me profoundly. And thanks to the two of them I've been mired in my own internal debate about the morality of utilizing violence in the name of self-defense and liberation. To this day I remain conflicted about this issue. I see the value in Gandhi's moral arguments and I do feel that as individuals and societies we must ultimately rise above violence if we are to live in a just and peaceful world. However, if an armed intruder broke into my home and threatened to kill my family and the only option I had to prevent their slaughter was to resort to violence, then I would probably feel justified in resorting to violence. And if violence is justifiable on a personal level to save a life, doesn't the same justification also apply to the defense of many lives?

Ultimately, it is only when we encounter the most extreme of challenges that we can be certain of our moral fiber. And being a white middle-class male who lives in a wealthy nation in the global North, my privilege has helped protect me from having to face a challenge so extreme as to force me to decide whether or not violence is a morally acceptable response. However, I have met many people in Latin America who have been forced to endure levels of oppression and misery inconceivable to many of us in the global North, and I don't feel that I have the right to judge how they respond to their oppression. This is especially true given that I'm not sure how I would respond if I were in their position. Consequently, I cannot honestly claim to be a pacifist or even a committed advocate of non-violence, even though I believe in both the overall idealism of Gandhi's moral principles and the fact that there are very few situations in which the use of violence can be justified. For me, violence must only be used as a last resort.

CHAPTER 8

Death at Home and Abroad

With my Political Science degree requirements completed, and my moral dilemma regarding violence and non-violence an ongoing internal debate, I graduated from UNLV in June 1999. I became a US citizen at the same time; in actuality, I was a dual citizen because I retained my British citizenship. Jacqui and I returned home to New York in August and moved back into our old apartment in the East Village. I got a job with the North American Congress on Latin America (NACLA) as a part-time editorial assistant for its bi-monthly magazine *NACLA Report on the Americas*. I didn't realize when I began working at NACLA that my life was about to become intimately linked to the US war on drugs in Colombia.

In January 2000, US President Bill Clinton announced a new multi-billion dollar counter-narcotics initiative called Plan Colombia, making Colombia the third-largest recipient of US military aid after Israel and Egypt. Within a week of Clinton's announcement I launched an online publication called *Colombia Report* (renamed *Colombia Journal* in 2003) with the goal of informing the US public about its government's escalating role in Colombia's armed conflict. I felt that by investigating the escalating US military intervention in Colombia I could in some small way make amends for my failure to question the US role in El Salvador following my release from prison in that country. The title of the first article I penned for *Colombia Report* asked, "Are We 'Salvadorizing' Colombia?"

I quit NACLA in June 2000 and decided to work exclusively as an investigative journalist covering the US intervention in Colombia. I saw my role as a journalist as part of the broader social justice movement, investigating issues related to US foreign policy and neoliberal globalization in order to provide information that activists could then use in their efforts to organize. I viewed my role in providing information as one link in the activist chain, which included other people engaged in solidarity, lobbying, protests and various other strategies and campaigns related to achieving social justice.

Because the perspectives of the Colombian government, the military and the US embassy dominated mainstream US media coverage of the conflict, I decided to conduct almost all of my field work in Colombia's rural conflict zones in an attempt to present those views that rarely received exposure. I wanted to investigate how the violence was affecting poor rural Colombians who lived in the conflict zones. I wanted to understand the socio-economic conditions that had led so many Colombian farmers to become dependent on the cultivation of coca—the plant that provides the raw ingredient in cocaine. And I sought to probe behind the headlines of the mainstream media, which repeatedly failed to provide any analysis of the political, social and economic problems that lay at the root of the conflict.

It seemed to me that Plan Colombia constituted a military implementation of neoliberalism in order to facilitate access to the country's extensive natural resources for multinational oil and mining companies. Most of Colombia's abundant oil and mineral reserves were situated in rural regions controlled by Marxist guerrillas belonging to the Revolutionary Armed Forces of Colombia (FARC). My suspicions about the escalating US intervention in Colombia were supported by statements made by US energy secretary Bill Richardson during his visit to the Colombian port city of Cartagena in 1999. Richardson clearly outlined US economic interests in the South American country when he declared, "The United States and its allies will invest millions of dollars in two areas of the Colombian economy, in the areas of mining and energy, and to secure these investments we are tripling military aid to Colombia." Within months of his statement it became apparent that a newly-signed IMF loan deal and its corresponding neoliberal reforms were intended to create favorable investment conditions for multinational corporations. Meanwhile, Plan Colombia sought to establish the necessary security on the ground that would allow those companies to access natural resources situated in FARC-controlled territory.

By the end of the 20th Century, FARC guerrillas controlled 40 percent of Colombia's national territory, much of it sparsely-populated rural regions. The guerrilla group profited from the drug trade, mostly through taxing drug operations in rebel-controlled territory, including the operations of cocaine processors and large coca plantations. The FARC had not only been fighting the Colombian military for more than three decades, it also had to contend with another enemy that emerged in the early 1980s. The

Colombian military, drug traffickers, wealthy business people and the country's traditional landowning elite established paramilitary groups to defend their economic interests and to combat the guerrillas. The ideology of these right-wing death squads was dominated by a fanatical anti-communism. Consequently, they sought to rid Colombia of any perceived communist subversion. In the eyes of the paramilitaries, a subversive was any individual or group that sought to achieve social change, including those whose activities were non-violent. As a result, unionists, community leaders, teachers, students, leftist politicians, human rights workers, peasant and indigenous organizers, and many of those who lived in rebel-controlled regions became targets in a "dirty war" intended to defend the political, social and economic status quo.

During the 1990s, more than forty thousand Colombians were killed in the armed conflict. According to Colombian and international human rights groups, and even the US State Department's annual human rights reports, paramilitaries closely allied with the US-backed Colombian military were responsible for more than 75 percent of the country's human rights abuses, including an overwhelming majority of the massacres. And, according to Carlos Castaño, commander of the country's largest paramilitary organization, the United Self-Defense Forces of Colombia (AUC), 70 percent of his group's funding came from drug trafficking. The paramilitaries also received funding from multinational corporations operating in Colombia. For instance, Cincinnati-based Chiquita Brands International would plead guilty in US Federal Court in 2007 to funding a foreign terrorist organization. Chiquita admitted paying $1.7 million to the AUC between 1997 and 2004 in return for the paramilitaries protecting the company's banana-growing operations in northern Colombia from guerrilla attacks. This "protection" involved the killing of hundreds of peasants in the region.

Despite this human rights and drug trafficking reality, Plan Colombia focused its sights on the FARC's traditional strongholds in the south of the country. For many of the farmers in those regions, coca constituted the only viable cash crop due to a lack of infrastructure, which made it difficult to transport perishable food crops to distant markets. And given that 64 percent of rural Colombians lived in poverty, the income from coca was crucial for many farmers. But Plan Colombia was about to make those farmers the principal target in Washington's war on drugs.

I travelled to Colombia for the first time as a journalist in June 2000. I had no idea at that time that I would return regularly over the next thirteen years. I had anticipated witnessing human suffering and death during my work in Colombia's rural conflict zones. I had not, however, expected that sort of tragedy to hit me at home.

On December 21, 2000, my father suffered a massive heart attack. He fell into a coma and was put on life support. Jacqui and I immediately flew to Windsor, Ontario, where my parents had moved after my father was laid-off from Massey Ferguson. My father lay motionless in the hospital bed with a countless array of tubes and wires linking him to various machines. In a weird way, he actually seemed at peace. I would sit there at his bedside stroking his arm and telling him that I loved him. Obviously he was not capable of replying, but I told him how I felt about him anyway, because it made me feel better.

The decision was made to take him off life support and the doctor told us that my father might not die immediately upon being disconnected from the machine;

that his severely weakened heart might hang on for several hours or even days. We all went in to visit him one more time to say our final goodbyes before they disconnected him, just in case he did die instantly. But he didn't. And nobody warned us about how his body would react once unplugged from the life support system. I had expected him to maintain the same peaceful disposition after he was disconnected that he'd exhibited while attached to life support. But when I went in to sit with him I was shocked to find his entire body convulsing violently and to hear his loud and erratic breathing, as though he were gasping for breath. It was horrifying to see my father in such a state. It was also incredibly creepy because it seemed as though his body had been possessed by some alien force. My father died in the early hours of Christmas Eve; he was 67-years-old.

I was in a state of emotional shock following my father's death. It had all happened so suddenly, so unexpectedly. I assumed that I was in shock because I couldn't think of any other explanation for the fact that I could function so effectively each day. My rational mind told me that I should be feeling more pain, and that I should be expressing more emotions, but it seemed that I wasn't feeling the full impact of his death. And I didn't understand why not.

I was still in a state of shock when I arrived in Colombia one month later. I was there to investigate Plan Colombia's initial aerial fumigations that had targeted coca crops in Putumayo in the country's Amazon region. I met a photo journalist named Eros Hoagland and we decided to work together. Eros was from California and the son of war photographer John Hoagland, who was killed by the

Salvadoran army in 1984 while covering that country's civil war.

We drove to the town of La Hormiga and checked into the Five Stars Hotel, which didn't even come close to living up to its name. Upon our arrival we learned that fifteen peasants had been massacred the previous day in the nearby hamlet of Los Angeles. We also learned that six of the dead bodies had been taken to the nearby village of El Placer. Eros and I found a taxi driver willing to take us to the village, which was only fifteen minutes away and under the control of the paramilitaries. On the drive to El Placer we saw our first evidence of the aerial fumigations. Numerous fields along the road were full of dead corn stalks and yucca plants. Directly across the road from one fumigated cornfield were hundreds of green coca bushes, apparently untouched by the spraying.

When we reached El Placer we quickly located the cemetery. Eros and I entered and walked past rows of graves until we reached an open-faced building. An old man sat in a chair in the middle of the structure while several other people hung around whispering quietly to each other. None of them appeared to be mourning. The corpses of two men and one woman were lying on the cement floor waiting to be claimed by loved ones. We were told that relatives had already retrieved the other three bodies.

The corpse nearest the front of the building was that of a shirtless, skinny, middle-aged man dressed in baggy beige trousers. He had been shot in the side of the face. Next to him was the body of a short woman dressed in a blue tee-shirt. The bullet hole in her cheek made evident the cause of death. Most disturbing, however, was her rounded belly pushing out against the dirty blue tee-shirt. She was clearly in an advanced stage of pregnancy. I turned to one of the women nearby to confirm the obvious.

"Was she pregnant?" I inquired.

"Yes," she replied. "Eight months."

"Do you know her?"

"Not really," she said. And then, pointing to the shirtless corpse, explained, "They are a couple. They're from Ecuador and work as coca pickers. I don't think they have any family here."

"What will happen to their bodies if nobody comes to collect them?" I asked.

"They'll be buried in the ground at the rear of the cemetery."

I walked over to the third corpse. It was a large man dressed in a bright orange tee-shirt and blue jeans. His hands were tied together at the wrists with a white plastic bag. His face had been pummeled beyond recognition, caved in by repeated blows from a hammer, a large stone or some other blunt object. I turned to the old man and asked if he knew who had committed the massacre. He just shrugged his shoulders as if to say, "Who knows?"

"We heard that fifteen people were killed. Where are the other bodies?" I inquired.

"They haven't found them yet," he replied.

After taking several photos of the bodies, Eros and I made our way back to the car. I had never before seen corpses that were the result of violent deaths. I had anticipated feeling nauseous or something like that, but I didn't feel anything. I felt like I should have felt something, but I didn't.

Two days after the massacre, the army launched an operation to retrieve the remaining bodies. Eros and I accompanied an army patrol that was searching for corpses in the small hamlet where the massacre had occurred while other soldiers were stationed in the rainforest perimeter to defend against a guerrilla ambush. The homes in the hamlet were not particularly close together because each was surrounded by land used for grazing animals and cultivating crops. The hamlet was eerily deserted. Other than our patrol, there were no signs of life inside or outside the simple wooden houses spaced along the dirt road. There weren't even any animals left in the hamlet. Several houses had the acronym of the country's largest paramilitary organization "AUC" spray painted on the walls. It was difficult to imagine that only days earlier there had been more than two hundred and fifty men, women and children going about their daily lives there, cultivating their crops and caring for their animals. But now the hamlet was a ghost town.

As we walked along the dirt road a faint but rather unpleasant odor began to penetrate my nostrils. I tried to ignore it. We continued moving forward into the breeze that was carrying the increasingly powerful and pungent smell. A small group of soldiers was standing off to the left side of the road in front of a small, unpainted wooden house. One of them told us that a body had been discovered around the side of the house. As Eros and I made our way around the corner the smell became almost unbearable. It was by far the foulest and most disturbing odor I had ever experienced. It seemed to penetrate not only my nose, but every inch of my being. I suddenly realized that the oppressive stench was emanating from the decomposing corpse. After all, the body had been rotting in the tropical heat for more than three days.

Four soldiers holding bandanas over their noses were standing over the lower half of a body. When I first saw only two legs clad in jeans and sneakers, I thought that the corpse had been cut in half. But as I drew closer I realized that it had been shoved into a hole in the side of the hill and only the lower half was visible above ground. A small stream emanated from the hole and ran under the corpse before weaving its way through the grass and down the hillside. The body was that of a heavy-set man and the soldiers appeared to be in no hurry to remove him from the hole. Eros and I took several photos before moving upwind in an effort to escape the smell.

We returned to the corpse when a red pick-up truck carrying four male teenagers arrived on the scene. The army had called them in to retrieve the body and to take it to the cemetery in El Placer. The boys covered their faces with their shirts in an attempt to defend themselves from the foul odor. Two of them grabbed the legs of the dead man and pulled him out of the hole. His face was one of the most horrific sights I'd ever seen, causing a momentary unsettling of my stomach. His lips were massively swollen and his eyes bulged to the point that I couldn't help but wonder what was preventing them from popping out of their sockets. The hideous swollen lips and bulging eyes were reminiscent of the exaggerated features of a ghoulish cartoon figure. Furthermore, the skin on his face, as well as that on his hands and arms, was a pure white color and hanging loose as though it was two sizes too big for him. I surmised that the disfigurations resulted from a combination of the water and the heat.

The cause of death was not immediately apparent and the overbearing stench kept me from hanging around to conduct any further inspection of the body. The four boys picked up the corpse, carried it out to the road and laid it in the bed of the pick-up truck. After the body had been removed from the hamlet, Eros and I continued on with the patrol. We spent the next hour patrolling with the soldiers but didn't find any more bodies. Even though we were now upwind of where the corpse had been found, the smell still lingered in my nostrils. In fact, that odor would return to haunt me on and off for the next several days. I also could not rid myself of the horrific image of that dead body in the hole.

I left Colombia a week later feeling as though I was surrounded by death, both at home and abroad. But it wasn't until a month after I returned to New York that my emotions finally came to the surface. There were days when I would find myself sitting on the couch in my living room crying. At first I didn't understand why I was crying; the tears just seemed to come out of nowhere. But then I realized that thoughts of my father would always enter my mind during those emotional outbursts. And then I recognized that I was finally grieving the loss of my father. For the first time, the full impact of his death, of the fact that I would never see his face again, or hear his voice again, overwhelmed me. I was feeling an enormous emptiness, and there was nothing I could do about it but cry.

CHAPTER 9

The Day that Shook the World

On the morning of September 11, 2001, I was packing clothes into a bag in our lower Manhattan apartment preparing for an afternoon flight to Colombia. It was then that I heard the newscaster on the television announce that a plane had just crashed into one of the twin towers at the World Trade Center. After the news revealed that a second plane had struck the other tower, it became evident that it was no accident and so I set aside my packing to watch the television coverage. Shortly after the first tower of the World Trade Center collapsed, a neighbor knocked on the door and said that people were going up to the roof to watch what was happening, so Jacqui and I decided to join them.

People had gathered on the rooftops of buildings throughout the East Village, staring at the smoke billowing from the lone remaining tower a little more than a mile to the south. Suddenly, a huge cloud of dust began to rise up from the base of the tower, enveloping and obscuring the entire structure. Despite the distance, I could hear a deep rumble. As the giant cloud of dust began to dissipate, a collective gasp could be heard across the neighborhood.

The second tower had vanished. It was as though a magician had just removed his handkerchief and the object of focus had disappeared before the audience's eyes. As the world would soon find out, this act of terrorism was perpetrated by the Islamic extremist group al-Qaeda.

After the shock of seeing, or more accurately hearing, the second tower collapse had subsided, we suddenly realized that the attack might not be over. After all, at that point we had no idea what was happening. And if there were to be more attacks against Manhattan, then we could end up stranded without electricity and water services. Jacqui and I decided to head to the grocery store two blocks away to stock up on bottled water, candles and canned food. The streets appeared normal on our walk to the store. However, when we exited fifteen minutes later with our emergency supplies we were astounded by what we encountered. Avenue C was filled with evacuees from downtown Manhattan making their way on foot to the north. It was a surreal sight. Thousands of men and women, most of them dressed in suits and covered from head to toe in white dust, solemnly making their way to safety.

Jacqui and I took our supplies home and then stood staring at each other, not sure what to do. My flight to Colombia, along with all other flights, had been cancelled. We didn't feel like watching any more of the television coverage of the attack. After all, how many times could one watch the footage of those planes striking the towers? And it didn't feel right to just sit at my desk and work, as though nothing had happened. We decided to try and find a way to help in this time of crisis. We spent the next few hours trying to donate blood, but the donor centers were already over-stocked. So we purchased groceries and donated them to the rescue and aid stations.

When I awoke on the second morning after the attack I decided I had to do more to help. I made my way down to Ground Zero and volunteered in the search for survivors. The scene was one of utter devastation. Everything for several blocks around Ground Zero was covered in a fine grey-white dust. It was six inches deep in places, reminiscent of freshly-fallen snow. At Ground Zero, two piles of rubble standing about six stories high were all that remained of the twin towers, each of which had stood one hundred and ten stories tall. Two of the world's most identifiable architectural landmarks had been reduced to a mangled mess of concrete, steel and dust. Among the debris were thousands of pieces of paper and occasionally a recognizable item such as a computer monitor that had miraculously survived the collapse. More disturbingly, I also came across people's personal effects, including a child's backpack and torn pieces of photographs of victims' loved ones.

For the next twelve hours I worked on one of the many human chains that wound their way over the mounds of rubble from where the firefighters were burrowing into the debris in search of survivors back to the perimeter of the disaster zone. We passed bucket after bucket of concrete chunks and other debris along the line to waiting dump trucks. In the other direction, we passed items requested by the firefighters such as oxygen, water, power saws and body bags. We found no survivors. We also didn't find any bodies; only parts of bodies.

At nine o'clock that evening, I made my way out of Ground Zero and headed uptown to rendezvous with Jacqui at her brother's apartment near Bellevue Hospital, which happened to be one of the two trauma centers where survivors were to be taken. An hour later, as Jacqui and I walked out onto First Avenue to make our way home, half a dozen Latinos called out to us and ran in our direction. My clothes were still covered in the dust that permeated everything at Ground Zero, making it obvious where I'd been.

"Have you been down at Ground Zero?" one of them asked me.

"Yes," I replied.

"Did you find any survivors?"

The one asking the questions was a young man who appeared to be in his mid-twenties. Beside him stood a woman about the same age and several other men and women who looked to be in their late teens. Clearly, they were hanging around Bellevue Hospital hoping to hear news of a loved one who had been in the World Trade Center that fateful morning two days earlier. Their facial expressions exhibited a seemingly contradictory blend of hope and despair. And then I realized, I was the source of that hope.

"The rescue line that I was working on didn't find any survivors," I explained. "But there were many other lines working down there and I don't know if they found anyone or not."

In my heart I knew there were no more survivors, but I didn't have it in me to tell them that. I didn't know what to say to those people who were grasping at any straw. And then the man who had asked the questions suddenly felt compelled to tell me the story of their missing loved ones.

"My brother works with his fiancé in the restaurant on the one hundred and sixth floor," he began. "He moved here from Mexico a year ago. They're planning to get married in the spring."

I couldn't help but notice that he told their story using the present tense as though the full reality of the nightmare had not yet registered. No doubt speaking in the present tense helped keep his loved ones alive. I uttered the only words that I could think of saying at that moment.

"There are a lot of people down at Ground Zero working incredibly hard," I mumbled inanely. "If there are any survivors then I'm sure they'll find them."

With that, I wished them luck, turned and walked away feeling both physically and emotionally drained. All I could think about was the suffering that those people were enduring and the cruel reality that they were not going to achieve any sense of closure in the near future, if ever.

Nine days after the 9/11 attacks President George W. Bush announced to Congress and the nation that the United States was launching a global war on terror. He claimed that the United States was attacked because the terrorists hated American values and our way of life.

"They hate our freedoms—our freedom of religion, our freedom of speech, our freedom to vote and assemble and disagree with each other," he declared.

But based on my experiences in Latin America over the years I felt that Bush was misleading the American people. It wasn't the freedoms enjoyed by Americans that US critics hated; it was the foreign policies of the US government and the operations of US corporations that were the most significant contributing factor to anti-American attitudes. Salvadorans during the 1980s had nothing against the way of life enjoyed by the average US citizen living in Iowa, Texas or any other state. They did, however, have serious grievances against the United States for supporting a Salvadoran military that brutally repressed them. The indigenous people I'd met in the Ecuadorian Amazon knew absolutely nothing about the freedoms enjoyed by the American people, but they were seething at the actions of US oil companies operating in their traditional lands.

There was also plenty of anti-American sentiment in Colombia, particularly in the rural regions targeted by Plan Colombia's aerial fumigations. Again, this anger wasn't rooted in a hatred of US freedoms; it resulted from US government policies that destroyed the livelihoods of Colombian peasants without offering them any viable alternatives. I couldn't help but feel that, while these Latin Americans who despised US policies were unlikely to retaliate in the manner of the fanatics who committed those unjustifiable acts of violence on 9/11, their dislike and distrust of the United States was both understandable and shared by many people around the world.

In his speech, President Bush made it clear that it was not only Islamic terrorists that the United States would target in its new war. "Our war on terror begins with al-Qaeda, but it does not end there," Bush declared. "It will not end until every terrorist group of global reach has been found, stopped and defeated." It soon became apparent that Washington's principal non-Islamic target would be the FARC, despite the fact that the rebel group's military operations were conducted within the geographic borders of Colombia and posed no threat whatsoever to the United States. And just like that, the war on drugs and the war on terror in Colombia became, essentially, the same war.

In July 2002, the US Congress approved $128 million in counter-terrorism aid in addition to the funding for Plan Colombia. At the same time, the Bush administration announced that it was deploying seventy US Army Special Forces soldiers to the Arauca region of eastern Colombia as part of the war on terror. There was no coca cultivation in Arauca, nor any cocaine processing labs. There was, however, plenty of oil, and the most prominent company operating in the region was Los Angeles-based Occidental Petroleum. Occidental partly-owned and operated a pipeline that ran from its Caño Limon oil field to the Caribbean coast. The pipeline was bombed by guerrillas a record one hundred and seventy times in 2001, shutting it down for two hundred and forty days that year and costing the company $100 million in lost earnings.

The mission of the US Army Special Forces troops was to provide counterinsurgency training to the Colombian Army's 18th Brigade. The 18th Brigade's primary mission was to defend Occidental's oil field and pipeline against guerrilla attacks. The aid package meant that US taxpayers were paying $3.55 in security costs for every barrel of Occidental oil that flowed through the pipeline, which contrasted sharply with the 50 cents per barrel that the company was contributing to its own security.

The provision of US military aid to provide security for a US oil company operating in Colombia did not surprise me. After all, Plan Colombia had not only targeted coca crops but had also boosted security for multinational oil companies operating in the country. Lieutenant Colonel Francisco Javier Cruz was the commander of twelve hundred army troops stationed in the town of Orito, which was the hub of oil operations in the Putumayo region. When I asked the colonel if US military aid had provided security for oil companies, he replied, "Yes, we are conducting better operations now because we have tools like helicopters, troops and training provided in large part by Plan Colombia." And, in a region where armed actors routinely targeted the civilian population, Lt. Col. Cruz made clear his priority: "Security is the most important thing to me. Oil companies need to work without worrying and international investors need to feel calm."

In February 2003, British photojournalist Jason Howe and I headed to the town of Saravena in Arauca to investigate the deployment of the US soldiers. Just prior to our arrival, the Colombian army had arrested more than two thousand people and interrogated them at the local soccer stadium. The overwhelming majority of those detained were not terrorists; they were human rights workers, community leaders, teachers and unionists who were critical of the security and economic policies being implemented by the US-backed Colombian government.

During our time in Saravena, Jason and I observed the US soldiers providing counter-insurgency training to Colombian troops belonging to the 18th Brigade. We also accompanied a unit of heavily-militarized National Police, known as *carabineros*, through rebel-controlled barrios of Saravena. The carabineros had also been trained by US Army Special Forces.

One day I accidentally discovered that the Colombian army was using children as a means to gather intelligence on guerrilla activity. Local children, some as young as three years of age, would be brought to the army base every Thursday to participate in the "Soldier for a Day" program. Army psychologists dressed in combat fatigues would then determine which of the children had family members in the guerrillas and attempt to turn them into informers.

On the evening of our fourth day in Saravena the guerrillas launched a major attack against the National

Police base in the center of town. Jason and I left our hotel to investigate the battle and ended up being caught in the middle of the street fighting. In the darkness we couldn't make out who was firing at who or even in which direction, only that the shooting was all around us. We'd rush from doorway to doorway and whenever we approached an armed police officer we would whisper, "Periodistas! Periodistas! Journalists! Journalists!" in the hope that we wouldn't be mistaken for guerrillas. Because of the darkness, it was difficult to determine exactly what was happening. So after awhile we decided to make our way carefully back to our hotel where we rode out the remainder of the one-and-a-half hour battle, which ended when the army rolled into town in tanks. Interestingly, I hadn't felt any fear while Jason and I were on the street during the fighting. It wasn't until I was safely in the hotel that the realization of what had just happened hit me and I thought to myself, "Wow! That was intense."

The next morning Jason and I participated in a US Embassy-organized press junket, which typified how most foreign correspondents covered the rural conflict in Colombia. Official press junkets, regularly organized by the Colombian military and the US embassy, are a convenient way for correspondents based in Bogotá to visit remote rural regions affected by the armed conflict. The problem, however, is that the journalists are flown to a specific destination chosen by the authorities where they spend a few hours with government and military officials and get presented with a pre-packaged story. Inevitably, the official line dominates the published account.

Most of the mainstream media correspondents in Colombia seemed to view their journalistic responsibility in much the same way that *New York Times* reporter Judith

Miller did in the lead up to the war in Iraq. When asked why her articles often did not include the views of experts skeptical of the Bush administration's claims of weapons of mass destruction, Miller shockingly replied, "My job isn't to assess the government's information and be an independent intelligence analyst myself. My job is to tell readers of *The New York Times* what the government thought of Iraq's arsenal." In other words, she believed that her job was to be little more than a stenographer for the US government.

Following their normal *modus operandi*, correspondents from the largest daily newspapers in the United States, along with reporters from the *Associated Press* and *Reuters*, flew into Saravena with two US embassy officials. Jason and I met up with them on the army base and we all sat there and listened to the commander of the US Army Special Forces troops describe how they were training units of the 18th Brigade in counter-insurgency to help defend the civilian population from terrorists. We then witnessed Colombian troops put on an exhibition of the unconventional warfare tactics they had learned from their US advisors. Less than two hours after touching down in Saravena the reporters and embassy officials were back on the plane and returning to the relatively safe confines of Bogotá. The reporters never left the army base during their brief stay in Saravena and did not speak with anyone other than US government officials and US and Colombian army officers.

As expected, the next day many US media outlets published virtually identical articles describing the difficult but important job that US soldiers were performing in Colombia to combat terrorism. Obviously, the articles provided only one perspective on the deployment of US troops to the region, and that was the government's perspective. All in all, the Saravena stories were not the sort of front line investigative reporting that we are led to believe is routinely conducted by the US mainstream media.

No journalists from the mainstream media bothered to return to Arauca to investigate the consequences of the US military engagement. And those consequences proved deadly for Colombians. During the two years that the US soldiers were based in Arauca, the Colombian Army's 18th Brigade not only used its newly-acquired unconventional warfare skills against guerrillas, it also targeted civilians. In May 2003, paramilitaries and soldiers from the 18th Brigade entered the Betoyes indigenous reserve where they raped and killed a pregnant 16-year-old indigenous girl and then cut the fetus out of her stomach before disposing of her body in a river. Two other indigenous people were also killed and more than eight hundred forcibly displaced.

On August 21, soldiers from the army base in Saravena raided homes and arrested forty-two trade unionists, social activists and human rights defenders who were accused of being terrorists. Several months later, soldiers from various units of the 18th Brigade rounded up more than twenty-five opposition politicians in Arauca less than a week before local elections. Amnesty International accused the administration of President Alvaro Uribe of politicizing human rights, claiming, "A lot of it has to do with silencing those who campaign for human and socio-economic rights." The timing of the arrests, only days before local elections, also led an Amnesty spokesperson to declare, "It is part of a strategy to undermine the opposition's credibility."

In August 2004, Colombian soldiers from the same base housing the US military advisors again ventured out into Saravena's barrios. This time, the soldiers dragged three union leaders from their beds in the middle of the night and executed them in cold blood. The Colombian army initially claimed that the three unionists were armed guerrillas killed in battle. An investigation conducted by local and international human rights groups ultimately pressured Colombia's attorney general's office into launching its own probe. Deputy Attorney General Luis Alberto Santana later announced, "The evidence shows that a homicide was committed. We have ruled out that there was combat." In a rare case of justice being carried out in Colombia's dirty war, one army officer and two Colombian soldiers were arrested and charged with the murder of the three union leaders.

The Bush administration's expansion of the US military role in Colombia effectively turned US soldiers into Occidental Petroleum's personal security trainers. The efforts of the US Army Special Forces soldiers, who trained more than two thousand Colombian troops, paid dividends for the oil company as the Caño Limón pipeline was bombed only 17 times in 2004. The US advisors, however, had helped secure Occidental's operations by providing counterinsurgency training to a Colombian army brigade directly responsible for gross violations of human rights and for maintaining close ties to a right-wing terrorist group.

When I was in Saravena, I had asked one of the US Army Special Forces soldiers what he thought about paramilitaries entering villages and massacring suspected guerrilla sympathizers. "Sometimes that's what you have to do, I guess," he answered, without hesitation and with a nonchalant shrug of his shoulders. Given the atrocities that were being perpetrated by Colombian soldiers trained by US military advisors in Arauca, I couldn't help but think that US military aid was being used to wage a war of terror rather than a war against terror in order to protect the interests of a US oil company.

The human rights abuses being perpetrated by the US-backed Colombian military under the war on terror were not restricted to Arauca, they were occurring throughout the country. In 2002, when hardliner President Uribe was first elected, the Colombian state was responsible for 17 percent of the country's human rights violations. But four years later, at the end of Uribe's first term, the Colombian military was responsible for 56 percent of human rights abuses.

A significant component of those human rights violations became public in 2008 with the emergence of the "false-positives" scandal. The Colombian military was using civilian middle-men to go to the shantytowns of the country's cities to offer jobs to unemployed youth. The young men would be offered lucrative work in a rural region and then be taken there by bus. Upon arrival they would be handed over to the local army battalion, which would then execute the young men and pass them off as guerrillas killed in combat. One of the motivating factors for such systematic human rights abuses was the Colombian military's "body count" policy under which battlefield success against leftist guerrillas was largely measured by the number of rebels killed in combat. Incentives offered to military officers included extra leave, promotions, and cash rewards as high as $2,000 for dead guerrillas. Colombia's Attorney General's office is currently investigating more than 3,350 cases of extrajudicial executions perpetrated by Colombian army units throughout the country between 2002 and 2008. Disturbingly, de-classified State Department documents show that the US government was aware that false-positive killings were occurring long before it became public knowledge.

Many Colombians in rural regions continue to endure repression at the hands of the US-backed military with counter-insurgency operations being a major cause of forced displacement. With almost five million internally displaced people, Colombia has the world's largest internal refugee population. Not coincidently, most forced displacement has occurred in resource-rich regions as the military's counter-insurgency operations provide security for foreign investors. The overwhelming majority of foreign investment in Colombia has been in the resource extraction sector, with 80 percent of it in oil and mining. But while this investment has contributed significantly to economic growth, most of the wealth generated by this growth has left the country in the form of profits for multinational corporations. Meanwhile, the social consequences are not only evident in the country's human rights crisis, but also in the fact that Colombia was one of the only countries in Latin America to experience an increase in inequality during the first decade of the 21st century.

My work in Colombia made it increasingly apparent to me that my tax dollars were funding a military that was responsible for most of the country's violence and human rights abuses. Furthermore, the primary objective of the US military intervention in Colombia has not been to wage a war on drugs or terror, but to provide security for multinational corporations eager to take advantage of neoliberal reforms to gain access to the country's natural resources and cheap labor. And thanks in part to the mainstream media's failure to seriously question the legitimacy of the US role in Colombia, Washington has been able to carry out its military implementation of neoliberalism virtually unchallenged. In many ways, the US war on terror in Colombia mirrored the Bush administration's invasion of Iraq where neoliberal policies were also implemented and US corporations made huge profits under the guise of combating terrorism.

CHAPTER 10

The Home Front

Much of my work in Colombia has consisted of documenting the plight of the civilian population, particularly the rural poor, who have been the principal victims of the country's armed conflict. Perhaps more than anything else in my life, it's the things I've witnessed and experienced in Colombia's rural conflict zones that have humbled me to the point that I now find it impossible to remain indifferent to those who have suffered gross injustices. However, witnessing such hardship and human suffering was taking an emotional toll on me.

Sometimes when I returned home from working in Colombia people would ask me, "Don't you find the violence, poverty and suffering depressing?" At such times I would think of people like my friend Francisco Ramírez, the president of the Colombian state mineworkers' union, who continued to struggle for social justice even after surviving seven assassination attempts made against him because of his outspoken criticism of neoliberalism and the US military role in Colombia. I also thought of the many other courageous unionists, human rights workers, and indigenous and community leaders that I'd met over the years who were also bravely fighting for social justice. And I thought of all the Colombians who got up each morning and persevered because they didn't have the option of just walking away from it all. And I would answer, "Sometimes I get depressed, but mostly I feel inspired by those Colombians who struggle against such overwhelming odds and with such dignity to achieve the rights that so many of us take for granted."

But like so many others whose work involves dealing with violence and poverty in countries like Colombia, I would feel guilt. Often, when I returned home to the comforts of life in North America, part of me felt as though I didn't have the right to feel depressed or sad. After all, who was I to feel down given my privileged position in life? And while my rational mind knew that someone who did the work I did couldn't help but be affected by some of the traumatic experiences, it was still difficult to convince myself that I actually had the right to respond emotionally. And so I responded by bottling up my emotions.

At the same time that I was becoming increasingly emotionally engaged with the victims of Colombia's conflict, I was growing more and more disconnected from those closest to me back home in New York. I felt as though there wasn't anybody who could relate to my experiences in Colombia's war zones. Neither Jacqui or Steve, or anyone in my family, had ever experienced anything like my work in Colombia. And attempts to talk to people about my work usually elicited either effusive praise or accusations of stupidity for taking such risks, neither of which was particularly helpful. Consequently, I internalized my emotions and proceeded on auto-pilot in my interpersonal relationships. I didn't realize it at the time, but the trauma resulting from my father's death and the intensity of my work in Colombia were taking a psychological toll on me. And this state of affairs was proving particularly problematic for my marriage.

Jacqui had been very supportive of my desire to become a journalist. I was immensely grateful to her for providing me with both moral and financial support during my initial years as a journalist. But I began to realize that I was feeling suffocated in my work life and in our relationship. Jacqui's understandable concern for my safety in Colombia resulted in her trying to dissuade me from working in specific regions or investigating certain issues. But I felt compelled to go wherever the story took me. In short, I wasn't getting the sort of emotional support that I needed. But that wasn't Jacqui's fault; after all, she had no way of relating to my work, or perhaps I never really gave her the opportunity to be there for me. Regardless of the reasons, I was feeling increasingly disconnected from her. In fact, neither one of us was particularly happy with our marriage. But despite our issues, I never seriously considered leaving Jacqui. I believed that one way or another we would work through our problems. I was unaware at the time that my life was about to change dramatically yet again.

That change occurred in January 2003 at the World Social Forum in Porto Alegre, Brazil. I had been invited by Terry Gibbs, the new director of NACLA, to speak on a panel about race issues in Latin America. Terry and I had met a couple of times at meetings in New York during the previous few months. After one of those meetings, a group of us went out for food and drinks and Terry and I ended up engaged in a long conversation about her life. She was seven years younger than me and was born in Ontario, Canada to British parents. Her family moved to the Arctic

Circle when she was four-years-old and then to Wales when she was nine. Most of her formative years were spent in Wales before she moved back to Canada at fifteen to live in Calgary.

While the roots of my political awakening lay in my early experiences in Latin America, Terry's lay in the five months she spent living in rural Malawi in Africa as part of a Canada World Youth program when she was 21-years-old. She returned from Africa and became a political activist, having been affected by the poverty and oppression she witnessed in Malawi. She also returned to university in Calgary to obtain a BA in Political Science before getting her Master's and PhD in England. Terry's PhD dissertation was focused on El Salvador and Nicaragua and she spent one-and-a-half years living and working in those countries during the mid-1990s. She then worked in academia briefly before doing volunteer work in Palestinian refugee camps in Beirut, Lebanon. Upon her return to North America, she took the job at NACLA.

I was mesmerized by Terry's account of her life and the similarities to my own. We had both been raised apolitically in the same two cultures: Britain and North America. And we both felt like outsiders in those cultures. We both became politically engaged as a result of personal experiences in poor nations of the global South. And we both had travelled and worked extensively in difficult conditions in Latin America and had developed a passion for the region. I went home that evening intrigued by Terry.

Following our panel at the World Social Forum, Terry and I went out alone together. It was one of the most magical nights of my life. We stayed up all night in a bar talking about our personal lives and our work in great detail. I couldn't believe that I was having such an intimate conversation with someone who in one way was a virtual stranger, and yet in another felt like my oldest friend. We connected in an intense and powerful way, both emotionally and intellectually. It was an incredibly passionate night, even though kissing represented the only physical contact. Our conversation finally concluded at six o'clock in the morning because I had to leave for the airport to catch a flight to Colombia.

We walked out of the bar into the empty street. The sun was beginning to rise as we kissed each other goodbye. Terry began walking one way to her hotel and I went in the opposite direction in search of a taxi. As I was walking away I heard Terry's voice call out my name. I turned and saw her standing in the middle of the deserted street.

"What's going to happen when we get back to New York?" she yelled.

In my best Humphrey Bogart impersonation, I replied, "I don't know. But we'll always have Porto Alegre."

She smiled and, as I turned and walked away, I knew that I was in love with her.

During that trip to Colombia I could not stop thinking about Terry. But even though I was in love with her I couldn't imagine just walking away from a ten-year relationship with Jacqui. Furthermore, it had been, for the most part, a good ten-year relationship. I constantly went back and forth regarding what I should do when I returned to New York. One minute I decided that I would leave Jacqui, the next I would decide to tell Terry there was no way that we could enter into a relationship. The strong monogamous streak in me meant that having an affair was out of the question. It had to be either Jacqui or Terry. It was during that trip to Colombia that British photojournalist Jason Howe and I got caught up in the middle of the prolonged street battle in Saravena. I found myself not only relieved to have survived the battle, but surprised to discover that a great part of that relief was due to the thought of being able to see Terry again.

Telling Jacqui that I had met someone else was one of the most difficult things I'd ever had to do. Not so much because it was uncomfortable for me, which it was, but rather because I hated to hurt Jacqui. I still loved her, just not enough. After I had finished telling her, Jacqui asked me to leave immediately. I threw some clothes into a bag, headed out of the door and moved in with Terry.

While part of me felt distressed about the end of my marriage, another part of me felt liberated. In addition to the similar cultural backgrounds and paths that our lives had followed, Terry and I also shared almost identical political and philosophical views. We both believed that compassion for others, particularly those less fortunate than ourselves, was a crucial component of humanity, essential in both individuals and societies. We believed that meeting the basic needs of people around the world must take priority over the profit-taking of corporations and the consumer excesses of people living in the wealthy nations of the global North. Essentially, we believed that the exploitation of one person by another, and of one nation by another, had to end if we were ever going to achieve sustainable peace and social justice in this world.

CHAPTER 11

The Capitalist Genocide

In August 2004, Terry and I moved to Cape Breton Island in Nova Scotia, Canada. Terry's job as director of NACLA had largely consisted of administrative work, which she did not find particularly fulfilling, so she wanted to return to academia. Meanwhile, New York's high cost of living had never made it an easy place to survive as an independent journalist. So when Terry received notification of a job opening in the Department of Political Science at Cape Breton University, we decided she should apply. The university offered Terry the job and so we made the move. After living in the United States for twenty-nine years, I headed north to Canada and made the transition from New York City and its population of eight million to Sydney with its twenty-six thousand inhabitants. Due to my journalistic experience and publication record, the Department of Political Science offered me a part-time position teaching courses on international politics, which I gladly accepted.

Cape Breton proved to be not only geographically stunning, but historically fascinating due in part to a radical union movement that had emerged in response to the oppressive working conditions that existed in the local steel plant and coal mines during the early decades of the 20th century. More recently, the island had been negatively impacted by the process of neoliberal globalization as the steel plant and the last coal mine were closed in 2001. I quickly discovered that neoliberalism had ravaged Cape Breton in the same way it had devastated Detroit and other industrial regions in the United States. As a result, Cape Breton's economy in the early 21st century was marked by the loss of well-paid, unionized industrial jobs and the arrival of low-paid, non-unionized service sector work in call centers and box stores.

There were other similarities between Canada and the United States with regard to the impacts of neoliberalism. Inequality had increased over the previous fifteen years with the richest ten percent of Canadians enjoying a 24 percent increase in their income while the poorest ten percent endured an eight percent decline. The rich were getting richer, in part, because Canada was slashing the corporate tax rate from 29 percent to 15 percent and the reduced government revenues led to cuts in social spending, particularly education and health care. Meanwhile, many middle-class Canadians, like their US counterparts, were only able to maintain their standard of living by working more hours, having two people in a household work, and running up record-levels of personal debt.

Not long after arriving in Cape Breton I also discovered that my new home was intimately connected to Colombia. The last Cape Breton coal mine had closed because the province's privately-owned utility company, Nova Scotia Power (NSP), had taken advantage of neoliberal globalization when it began importing coal from Colombia in 1999. And so, through the Atlantic Regional Solidarity Network (ARSN), I became engaged in a campaign to raise awareness among the residents of Nova Scotia about the human rights abuses related to the Colombian coal being imported to generate electricity in the province.

ARSN was part of a broader international campaign working in solidarity with Afro-Colombian and indigenous villagers in the La Guajira region of northern Colombia who were being forcibly displaced from their lands by the expansion of the Cerrejón Mine, the world's largest open-pit coal mine, which was owned by three of the world's largest multinational mining companies.

The campaign was a response to the forced displacement of the Afro-Colombian village of Tabaco in August 2001. Two hundred soldiers, police and the mine's private security force oversaw the bulldozing of all the buildings and structures in the community, including the school and cemetery. The campaign sought to convince the multinational owners of the mine to negotiate a collective relocation of the displaced villagers of Tabaco and to commit to negotiating collectively with the villages to be displaced by future expansion. The villagers wanted a collective negotiation and relocation process in order to keep their social networks and communities intact. For its part, the mine preferred the Western cultural approach of holding negotiations with individual property owners, which allowed it to engage in a strategy of divide and conquer.

THE CAPITALIST GENOCIDE

I visited the communities affected by the mine on four occasions and learned that the indigenous Wayúu people had lived in the region for thousands of years while the Afro-Colombian communities had been founded by escaped slaves whose descendants had lived in the area for generations. Indigenous Wayúu and the Afro-Colombian communities were engaged in subsistence farming that included cultivating crops, raising goats and chickens, and hunting and fishing. The arrival of the giant coal mine displaced more than 1,100 Wayúu during the 1990s and its expansion required the displacement of more communities in the early 21st century. The mine didn't even generate employment for local villagers; all of the mine's workers were brought in by bus from distant cities.

In response to a growing public campaign and increased media coverage of the issue, NSP agreed to meet with Tabaco community leader José Julio Pérez when we brought him to Nova Scotia in March 2006. NSP representatives met with Pérez in a luxurious boardroom—by rural Colombian standards—on the sixteenth floor of the company's headquarters in Halifax. Despite the fact that José Julio was an impoverished Colombian peasant who, along with his wife and four children, had been homeless for the previous five years after being forcibly displaced by the Cerrejón Mine, an NSP representative had the audacity to open the meeting by callously stating that the company's principal concern was its public image. NSP representatives then listened to José Julio state his community's case, but the company ultimately refused to use its leverage as a customer to publicly pressure the mine's owners into negotiating a collective relocation with the displaced residents of Tabaco. NSP's response did not come as a surprise since a company spokesperson had previously told me, "Nova Scotia Power does not become involved in human rights issues in the countries from which it purchases coal. The company is only concerned with two things: price and quality."

The harsh reality experienced by José Julio and the other displaced residents of Tabaco closely reflected that of millions of other Colombians who have been forcibly displaced so that the natural resources on their lands could be exploited for corporate profit and to support our privileged lifestyles in the global North. Meanwhile, when the coal reserves in La Guajira expire in twenty years, the mining company will simply up and leave, as the oil company had done in the indigenous village that I'd visited in the Ecuadorian Amazon in 1989. And, as with the devastation wrought on that indigenous community, Wayúu and Afro-Colombian communities in La Guajira will undoubtedly find their lands uninhabitable and their culture decimated.

In her analysis of rural communities that have been impacted by neoliberal globalization, Indian physicist and philosopher Vandana Shiva has argued that the capitalist concept of development doesn't reduce poverty, it actually causes poverty. She claims that the materialistic standard of living that exists in the wealthy nations of the global North is not possible for everyone on the planet, therefore it is a false measurement of development. So while billions of people like the Colombian villagers in La Guajira might not possess the same luxury goods as people in wealthy nations, as long as they have access to land they can meet their basic needs. Consequently, according to Shiva's argument, they are not poor. But when multinational corporations displace them from their lands in the name of profit and economic growth, they then lose the capacity to meet their basic needs and become truly poor.

From its inception capitalism has been a global colonial system dependent on exploiting the cheap labor and natural resources of the global South to generate profits for capitalists and to support the relatively privileged lifestyles of people in the global North. This process has resulted in gross global inequalities with the wealth gap between the global North and the global South growing from a factor of 3:1 in 1820 to 35:1 in 1950 to 72:1 in 1990 and to 167:1 in 2010. Vandana Shiva explains how this growing inequality has historically occurred under capitalism:

> The poor are not those who have been 'left behind'; they are the ones who have been robbed. The riches accumulated by Europe are based on riches taken from Asia, Africa and Latin America. Without the destruction of India's rich textile industry, without the takeover of the spice trade, without the genocide of the native American tribes, without Africa's slavery, the Industrial Revolution would not have led to new riches for Europe or the US. It was this violent takeover of Third World resources and markets that created wealth in the North and poverty in the South.

The process described by Shiva continues today under neoliberal globalization because the logic of capitalism compels corporations to constantly expand their operations around the globe in order to increase profits and accumulate more and more wealth under the mantra of economic growth. This constant expansion requires the commodification of virtually everything. In other words, nothing has value until it enters the market. Shiva points out that, under capitalism, "if you consume what you produce, you do not really produce, at least not economically speaking. If I grow my own food, and do not sell it, then this does not contribute to GDP [Gross Domestic Product], and so does not contribute towards 'growth'." Consequently, under the logic of capitalism, those who engage in traditional and sustainable forms of production must be incorporated—often by force—into the global capitalist system.

This is precisely why the forced displacement of the indigenous Wayúu and Afro-Colombian communities in La Guajira contributes to economic growth and is, therefore, viewed as "development" or "progress." Their subsistence farming culture meant that they consumed most of what they produced, therefore it was not sold on the market, which meant it did not contribute to the country's GDP. Consequently, under capitalist logic, these people are not engaged in productive activities even though they have supported themselves in an environmentally sustainable manner for generations.

The forced displacement of the Wayúu and Afro-Colombians from their lands has allowed multinational corporations to extract coal and trade it on the global market, thereby ensuring that the value of that coal contributes to Colombia's GDP. Furthermore, displaced farmers are now forced to purchase the food and other basic goods that they previously produced for themselves, further contributing to the nation's GDP.

The forced displacement of peasants from their traditional and sustainable lifestyles contributes to economic growth and increased profits for multinational corporations while simultaneously ensuring the relatively luxurious lifestyles of all of us in the global North—and this process constitutes capitalist development. It is a process that Karl Marx identified one hundred and fifty years ago and labelled "primitive accumulation." According to Marx, "The expropriation of the agricultural producer, of the peasant, from the soil, is the basis of the whole [capitalist] process. The history of this expropriation assumes different aspects in different countries, and runs through its various phases in different orders of succession, and at different historical epochs."

The plight of the Wayúu and Afro-Colombians in La Guajira highlights how the profits of multinational corporations and the functioning of the global capitalist system are dependent on violence, exploitation, poverty, inequality and ecological destruction. Meanwhile, governments and many non-governmental organizations (NGOs) in the global North funnel "aid" and "charity" to the global South in a vain attempt to alleviate some of the suffering caused by our wealth-generating activities. But as Shiva has said in reference to the "aid" and "charity" provided by us to the poor in the global South, "It's not about how much more we can give, so much as how much less we can take."

Shiva's statement really hit home for me. For many years my investigations in Colombia and my experiences in other parts of Latin America had repeatedly revealed to me that US policy and the operations of multinational corporations were about exploiting the region's labor force and natural resources both for profit and to sustain our comfortable lifestyles in North America. Salvadorans work as virtual slave laborers in maquiladoras making designer clothing for us to wear. Many of those Salvadorans who aren't lucky enough to find a job are forced to live the precarious life of an illegal immigrant in the United States. Mexican farmers who had been able to meet their basic needs for thousands of years have been displaced by NAFTA with many of them joining their Salvadoran *compañeros* in the exodus to the United States. And Colombian farmers are either having their precious food crops fumigated with chemicals or are being forcibly displaced because their lands sit on resources desired by multinational corporations. In all of these cases, poverty and inequality have increased because of our need to keep "taking more."

The capitalist system as defined by the WTO, IMF, World Bank and trade agreements such as NAFTA has been structured to ensure that we in the global North can keep taking and taking from the poor in the global South. While corporate profits and stock market indexes have increased dramatically in recent decades under neoliberalism, millions of people in the global South have endured violence, forced displacement, poverty and growing inequality. But as Shiva pointed out, this is not a new phenomenon, it has been the reality throughout the history of capitalism.

My experiences in Colombia led me to research other countries in more depth and I discovered that hundreds of millions of people around the world had been forcibly displaced by capitalist "development" during previous decades. Many of them became engaged in a desperate struggle for survival because the rate of rural displacement far exceeded the rate of urban job creation. The lack of formal sector employment has forced people to engage in the "informal economy" in cities throughout the world. As a result, many are forced to grovel daily through garbage in municipal dumps in search of anything of value to sell on the streets. According to the United Nations, the percentage of the economically active population in the global South engaged in the informal sector has almost doubled in recent decades from 21 percent in 1970 to more than 40 percent. This massive forced displacement of rural populations and destruction of local cultures has also contributed to increased levels of violence and crime, including prostitution, human trafficking and terrorism. It has also led to massive migrations of peoples as economic refugees desperately seek ways to survive. Meanwhile, millions of others just die.

In the early 21st century, more than half a million women die each year as a result of complications with pregnancy and childbirth, and 99 percent of these deaths occur in the global South. As one United Nations report explains, "Almost all of these deaths could be prevented if women in developing countries had access to adequate diets, safe water and sanitation facilities, basic literacy and health services during pregnancy and childbirth." Additionally, according to the World Health Organization, 1.6 million people worldwide died of AIDS in 2012, with 1.2 million of the deaths occurring in Sub-Saharan Africa. Meanwhile, according to a study commissioned by the World Health Organization and UNICEF, six million children die annually before reaching their fifth birthday due to preventable or treatable diseases such as diarrhea, pneumonia and malaria. Almost half of these child deaths occur in Sub-Saharan Africa.

In total, according to the World Health Organization, more than ten million people in the global South die annually from preventable and treatable diseases. They are victims of "structural violence" because, as medical anthropologist Paul Farmer has stated, their "social status denies them access to the fruits of scientific and social progress." In other words, the structures of the global capitalist system ensure that certain social groups accumulate great wealth while others are deprived of their basic needs. Such inequality is rooted in the logic of capitalism, which compels capitalists to prioritize profits and wealth accumulation over everything else, including basic human well-being.

At the beginning of the 21st century, the United Nations Development Program (UNDP) highlighted global inequality in a way that made apparent the consequences of structuring the world according to the logic of capitalism. An additional $6 billion a year would have ensured that all children in the global South received a basic education, meanwhile, $8 billion was being spent annually on cosmetics in the United States. Similarly, Europeans spent

$11 billion a year on ice cream, $2 billion more than the amount required to provide safe drinking water and adequate sanitation for everyone in the South. And the $17 billion that Americans and Europeans spent annually on pet food would easily have provided basic health care for everyone in the South.

Such a degree of global inequality is not simply an unintended consequence of capitalism; it is an essential component of the global capitalist system. After all, from the perspective of corporations, there are billions of dollars in profits to be made selling cosmetics, ice cream and pet food to North Americans and Europeans, whereas there is no viable market for education, health care and safe drinking water in the global South where the majority of people simply cannot afford to pay for them. Therefore, decisions that prioritize the production of luxuries for consumers in the global North over necessities for people in the global South are not simply callous choices; they are perfectly "rational" business decisions made according to the logic of capitalism. But prioritizing the production of these luxuries is only part of the problem; the system also requires consumers to purchase the products. Therefore, all of us consumers in the global North are complicit in the structural violence that needlessly causes the deaths of more than ten million people annually.

Capitalists and their political lackeys claim that the worldwide establishment of neoliberalism will ultimately bring the relatively luxurious lifestyles enjoyed by most of us in the global North to everyone on the planet. In other words, it is suggested that by continually achieving economic growth, all children will not only have access to a basic education, they will also be able to beautify themselves with cosmetics to the same degree as people in the United States. That not only will everyone in the global South have safe drinking water and adequate sanitation, they will also be able to indulge in ice cream on a scale equal to Europeans. And in addition to having basic health care, everyone will be able to spoil their household pets in the same manner as Americans and Europeans. But such a reality is not possible. We would need more than four planet Earth's to provide the necessary resources for seven billion people to enjoy a lifestyle equal to that currently enjoyed by most in the wealthy nations of the global North.

The global capitalist system has also been dependent from its inception on fossil fuels, particularly coal and oil, and we are just now beginning to come to terms with the dire environmental consequences of this reality. But the logic of capitalism is blind to the ecological crisis that has resulted from the prioritization of the pursuit of profit over all else. In order to maximize profits and generate ever-increasing amounts of wealth, capitalism requires constant economic growth. But while capitalism's inherent need for growth is infinite, the planet's natural resources are finite. Consequently, the contradiction in the capitalist system becomes apparent because economic growth can only occur through increased production of goods, all of which require the exploitation of natural resources. Therefore, capitalism cannot effectively address the environmental crisis it creates because its constant need to expand in order to generate profits and wealth is dependent on destroying nature.

One potentially catastrophic environmental consequence of capitalist development is global warming. And as with so many other aspects of capitalism, inequality is prevalent with regard to who will be most negatively impacted by this emerging crisis. While it is the wealthy capitalist nations that are responsible for the overwhelming majority of greenhouse gas emissions that have caused global warming, it is the nations of the global South that are going to bear the brunt of the consequences because many of them are located in tropical regions that will be the most negatively impacted. As Kermal Dervis of the United Nations Development Program (UNDP) pointed out, "Ultimately, climate change is a threat to humanity as a whole. But it is the poor, a constituency with no responsibility for the ecological debt we are running up, who face the immediate and most severe human costs." Furthermore, the unequal distribution of the planet's natural resources not only generates inequality between the haves and the have-nots today, it also results in inequality between the haves of today and the have-nots of tomorrow because we are consuming the resources that belong to future generations.

I cannot count the number of times that I've heard people in the global North argue that over-population is the primary cause of poverty, resource scarcity and global warming. The solution, they say, is to address population growth in the poor nations of the global South. In other words, if those people would simply stop having babies then there would be sufficient resources for us to maintain our privileged lifestyles in the global North and to save the planet. It is a "blame the poor" approach to the issue that denies the root causes of the problem.

For instance, if we were to eliminate the poorest three billion people on the planet it would have virtually no impact on the amount of natural resources consumed or the level of greenhouse gases emitted. These people simply do not consume any resources of significance nor do they generate much pollution. However, if we were to eliminate the wealthiest half a billion people living in North America and Europe then there would be plenty of resources left for the remainder of the world's population and the threat of global warming would be significantly diminished. The problem isn't over-population, it's the fact that privileged people in the global North are consuming more than their share of the planet's resources at an unsustainable rate. If people want to link population to diminishing resources and global warming then they should point the finger at privileged people in wealthy nations, not the poor in the global South.

The more I investigated the realities of global capitalism, the more I understood that it is a social system that is authoritarian to the core. How can it not be? The prioritization of individual rights, particularly the right to private property (i.e. private sector ownership of the economy), ensures that a small percentage of the world's population owns the means of generating wealth and any attempt to threaten their privilege inevitably results in a violent response though government repression, economic sanctions or military intervention.

I came to realize that, in spite of everything I'd been told my entire life, capitalist society cannot be a democratic society. The concept of "democracy" in a capitalist society exists solely in the political sphere, while the economy is managed in an authoritarian manner according to the logic of capitalism. In a capitalist society, workers are required to surrender their democratic rights and most of their individual freedoms every time they enter the workplace. Therefore, many of us spend most of our waking hours in an authoritarian job structure, where we don't have a meaningful voice in the major decisions that impact our lives.

Most people who have internalized capitalist concepts of democracy would never advocate for a dictatorship in the political sphere, regardless of how benevolent it may be. And yet, as employees, they unquestioningly tolerate dictatorship in the economic sphere of their lives, whether benevolent or not. The resulting disempowerment and alienation leaves workers with little recourse for achieving fulfilment in their life other than through the temporary gratification they get from consumerism, including the excessive consumption of alcohol, illegal drugs and anti-depressants.

By now it had become glaringly apparent to me that the global inequality in power and wealth that results in structural violence is maintained through imperialist structures that ensure crucial policymaking is conducted by governments in the global North and un-democratic international institutions such as the WTO, IMF and World Bank that serve the interests of corporations. As a result, there exists a democratic deficit in which a majority of the world's population has little or no say in the major decisions that directly impact their lives.

The lack of input into policymaking and the inability to access land, food and life-saving drugs sentences more than ten million people to death each year. Given the huge number of people who die annually as a result of conscious actions adhering to the logic of capitalism, I determined that the structural violence inherent in capitalism constituted a "structural genocide." More precisely, I concluded that capitalism constitutes a class-based structural genocide, with the principal victims being the poor in the global South. And this global catastrophe became the focus of my seventh book, titled *Capitalism: A Structural Genocide*, which was published in 2012.

CHAPTER 12

From Fatherhood to Socialism

Upon moving to Cape Breton I began a seven-year stretch during which I wrote six books while still managing to spend one or two months annually conducting investigative journalism in Colombia. Also, at the age of forty-six, I became a father. On April 24, 2006, our son Owen was born and I cannot describe the pure joy that I felt. Terry and I decided that we didn't want Owen to be an only child and so, on September 18, 2008, our second son Morgan was born. Terry and I were ecstatic.

I quickly came to realize that parenthood, the most natural life experience for human beings, was also the most exhilarating experience in life. It seemed ludicrous that I had not wanted children when I was younger because I selfishly believed that they'd infringe upon my freewheeling lifestyle. Thankfully, my feelings about becoming a father shifted as I got older. I'd lived an exciting life full of amazing experiences but not one of them remotely compared to that of being a father. For years I listened to parents tell me about the wonder of having a child and I would dismiss them as people who simply didn't understand how full and rich my life was. But I finally realized that it was I who didn't understand how amazing and magical their lives were. Our life with two small children was nothing less than wonderful and I went about my work both in Colombia and at home with my nuclear family constituting the center of my universe. Little did I know that my family was about to suddenly increase in size again.

In December 2010 I discovered that I had a daughter in Panama. She had located me through the Internet, which was not difficult because I had a significant online presence due to my journalism work. Her name was Johan and she was 29-years-old. Johan also had a two-year-old daughter named Kathleen. I was a grandfather! Johan described her mother to me and various personal details about me and my family that she had learned from her mother. I thought back to my Marine Corps days in Panama and, based on Johan's birthday, realized that she'd been conceived less than two months before the relationship I had with her mother had ended, which was just prior to my departure from Panama.

Terry handled this new discovery with amazing understanding and compassion, unquestioningly accepting that Johan and Kathleen were going to be part of our family. And two months after receiving that initial email, Terry and I flew to Panama to meet the newest members of our family. It was a powerful emotional experience. Johan and I had long talks and began to get to know each other. Her mother had never married and had raised Johan and her brother single-handedly, working as a domestic servant for most of her life and surviving in difficult economic circumstances. The following year Terry and I took Owen and Morgan to Panama and we spent a magical ten days with the whole family together. All of a sudden, I had a more intimate connection to Latin America than I'd ever imagined possible.

Johan has since had a second child named Dylan and is now a single mother struggling in a country where unemployment is high and most jobs, if one is lucky enough to have one, pay poverty-level wages. The hardships that I'd witnessed in Latin America for so many years are now a reality for a member of my own family. And so we provide Johan, Kathleen and Dylan with financial support and fly to Panama every year to visit them.

In a way, my adult life has come full circle. My time in the Marines in Panama constituted my introduction to Latin America and now I was returning to that country regularly to visit family. Before visiting Johan for the first time, I hadn't been in Panama since 1989, three weeks before the US bombing and invasion. During my recent trips there I have discovered the degree to which neoliberalism has impacted the poor in that country. Foreign investment has not only arrived in the form of Canadian mining companies, which has resulted in violent confrontations with indigenous communities determined to defend their lands and ways of life, but also in the form of real estate and financial investment. Panama City now has an impressive oceanfront skyline that compares with Manhattan. But behind the city's glittering modern façade is the displacement of poor families from the old colonial section of the city.

The US bombing in 1989 caused significant damage to buildings in the colonial neighborhood of Casco Viejo because that is where the presidential palace and headquarters of the National Guard were located. The US military's targeting of Manuel Noriega killed thousands of poor people and destroyed the homes of many others who lived in that neighborhood. During the following decade, foreign investors took advantage of the abandoned buildings by maintaining the colonial façades and renovating the interiors into luxury condominiums. Not surprisingly, this process drove up real estate prices in Casco Viejo as it was transformed into an upper-class neighborhood and a tourist attraction filled with boutique hotels and restaurants.

Slowly, poor families who had lived in the neighborhood for generations were being forced out and many of them have been relocated to housing projects outside of the city where there are no jobs, little public transportation and few amenities such as stores. They have been removed to an isolated location so that wealthy Panamanians and foreigners are not inconvenienced by their presence. Neoliberalism in Panama was initiated by US militarism, which paved the way for extensive foreign investment in real estate and mining.

Being a parent caused me to become even more focused on the sort of world we live in and what kind of future it holds for my children and grandchildren. And so, in conjunction with critiquing capitalism, I also began to reflect more expansively on potential alternatives. It seemed to me that the obvious solution to the economic authoritarianism inherent in capitalism was to achieve economic democracy through what Karl Marx called the social ownership of the means of production. In other words, the economic production process should be democratically-determined by the workers and the workers should own the products of their labor. Such an economic democracy, in conjunction with a grassroots political democracy, would allow people to have democratic control over every sphere of their lives. In other words, it would provide people with a meaningful voice in all of the major decisions that impact their lives.

In an economic democracy people would have a meaningful voice in all decisions made in the workplace related to wage levels, benefits, hours, workload, work assignments, working conditions, and the production and distribution of the goods and services produced. The resulting sense of empowerment would not only impact a person's life at work but also at home since many stresses in our non-work life such as finances, amount of leisure time and the general lack of control over our lives are related to our jobs. Ultimately, social ownership of the means of production constitutes an essential component of a participatory democracy.

One model of social ownership, and the most preferable in my mind, consists of worker-owned cooperatives. All workers would be co-owners and have equal decision-making power in how their workplace functions. However, it is crucial that there be some over-arching guidance through a participatory democratic process that ensures such entities produce in accordance with the needs of the community and the broader society. Otherwise this system could simply replace competition for profit between privately-owned businesses with competition for profit between cooperatively-owned enterprises. A society rooted in economic democracy and a grassroots political democracy represents a truly democratic socialism that would prioritize the well-being of everyone over profit for a few. Such a model would be distinctly different to the authoritarian socialism, or "communism," that existed in the Soviet Union.

But while I had come to believe that the idea of socialism made more sense than capitalism from a democratic, moral and humanitarian perspective, I also felt it was important to examine socialism in action rather than solely in theory. And so, in 2005, I made the first of many visits to Venezuela and Cuba to investigate the socialist models being implemented in those countries and to compare them to capitalist Latin American countries such as Colombia.

Like many other nations in the global South, Venezuela implemented neoliberal reforms during the 1980s and 1990s that contributed to an increase in the country's poverty levels. Venezuelans sought an alternative and, in December 1998, they elected Hugo Chávez to the presidency with 57 percent of the vote—the largest percentage total in four decades of Venezuelan democracy. Upon assuming office, Chávez immediately set about fulfilling his campaign promises to establish a new constitution and to implement policies that would ensure all Venezuelans and not just rich elites and foreign companies benefited from the country's oil wealth.

On one visit to Venezuela, Terry and I met with Lisandro Pérez, a community leader in one of the largest poor neighborhoods in the capital city of Caracas. Lisandro had been a community leader for decades and he told us that previous governments routinely deployed police to the community to repress grassroots organizing. But with the election of Chávez, they had a government that supported community-based initiatives.

The objective of Venezuela's Bolivarian revolution has been to create a new socialism, a grassroots socialism, which is different from the centralized socialism so prominent in the 20th century. This change cannot come from above, Lisandro explained, it must be rooted in local communities. According to Lisandro, "When the Berlin

Wall fell, we thought it was the fall of socialism, but that wasn't true. What was the significance of the fall of the Berlin Wall? In reality, it was the fall of the old models, the old orthodoxy, and something new was rising. It had to fall so that a new political project could rise."

Through our work in Venezuela, Terry and I soon learned that, despite the media's frequent portrayals of Chávez as an authoritarian leader who governed in an undemocratic manner, the social transformation underway in the country has not been authoritarian; in fact, it has been primarily rooted in participatory democracy. The central components of this participatory democracy consist of worker-owned cooperatives, communal councils, and direct democracy through national referendums.

A crucial aspect of Venezuela's revolution and participatory democracy has been the emergence of economic democracy through worker co-management of state-owned industries and the creation of more than 100,000 worker-owned cooperatives consisting of more than 1.5 million workers—18 percent of the nation's workforce. Agricultural cooperatives have been formed in the countryside as well as in urban areas alongside manufacturing cooperatives, with the principal objective being a shift of ownership of the means of production away from a minority of capitalist elites and into the hands of the broader population.

The cooperatives have emerged in conjunction with the creation of more than 40,000 communal councils in neighborhoods that seek to empower people at the grassroots level by allowing communities to devise and implement their own infrastructure and development projects. The communal councils receive funding from different levels of government, remain autonomous, and have extensive control over local decision-making. They are hugely popular because their small size (150–400 households) means that people have a meaningful voice in the decisions that most directly impact their lives. In addition to being vehicles for economic and participatory democracy, the cooperatives and communal-councils also seek to increase national self-sufficiency through local production for local consumption.

Terry and I visited one worker-owned cooperative that produced textile goods in a poor neighborhood in Caracas. The state oil company PDVSA had provided an interest-free loan to the cooperative, which was established by two hundred and eighty women from the local community. The women used the funding to construct a building using local labor and to purchase the necessary machinery and materials to begin producing clothing, bags and other textile products. The cooperative was providing inexpensive uniforms to schools and the military, and selling its other products to stores and vendors around Caracas. The textile workshop was bright and airy while the employees were full of good humor and positive energy. It was a far cry from the squalid sweatshops so prevalent in the global South that produce name-brand clothing for US and European designers. Furthermore, membership in the cooperative has allowed previously marginalized women to achieve a sense of empowerment. As member Louisa Ruiz proudly declared to us, "We are no longer staying in the house; we are business women now."

Ensuring that all citizens have free and equal access to quality health care and education has been a primary objective of the Venezuelan government's social policies, which have also been funded by the country's oil wealth. In the neoliberal era, the under-funded public education system in Venezuela was deteriorating while enrolment in private schools of children from the middle and upper classes increased steadily. Many poor families could not afford to send their children to school and so thousands were excluded from the system. In 1998, school enrolment consisted of only 59 percent of children. Over two million students had dropped out before grade six and another two million had failed to complete their secondary education. To address this crisis, the Chávez administration transformed the country's primary and secondary schools from traditional institutions into Bolivarian schools.

The Bolivarian schools contain kitchens staffed with parents from the community who have completed an intensive state-funded nutrition course. The school kitchens provide students with free breakfast, lunch and an afternoon snack in an attempt to lower the levels of malnutrition among poor Venezuelan children. Whereas many children had previously dropped out in order to the help their parents obtain food and other necessities, the provision of free meals have become an incentive to attend school. The Bolivarian schools also contain computer labs so all Venezuelan children and not only those from wealthy families can become computer literate in the 21st century.

Venezuela's public health system had also been ravaged by neoliberalism. It was seriously under-funded and not readily accessible to poor Venezuelans living in urban shantytowns and rural areas. For many poor Venezuelans, visiting a doctor meant travelling long distances followed by hours spent waiting in line. In 2003, in accordance with the new constitution's requirement that quality health care be freely accessible to all, the government launched Misión Barrio Adentro (Inside the Neighborhood Mission).

Under Barrio Adentro, neighborhood health committees have been formed so that citizens, particularly poor people, can participate in the development of health programs rather than being passive recipients of government policy. The committees are responsible for identifying their community's health needs and for contributing to the design and continuing evaluation of programs. The role of community members in taking responsibility for developing, managing and evaluating health care projects at the neighborhood level highlights the participatory nature of the democratic model emerging in Venezuela. It also illustrates how health care is both a right and a responsibility.

Because of a shortage of Venezuelan doctors willing to work in poor neighborhoods, Chávez began exchanging ninety thousand barrels of oil a day for ten thousand Cuban doctors, medical technicians, physical fitness trainers and literacy experts to staff the government's health and education missions. In other words, instead of engaging in the capitalist concept of a free-market trading system in which the principal actors are private corporations motivated by profit, Venezuela and Cuba are participating in a society-to-society barter trade process that ensures one country receives the doctors and educators it desperately needs while the other obtains the energy supplies it frequently lacks. In short, Venezuela has engaged in foreign policy and a trading system with its neighbors that are rooted in cooperation and solidarity rather than competition and exploitation. As a result of the Barrio Adentro mission, most Venezuelans now have a family physician located within a ten minute walk of their home.

The ongoing transformation to socialism has dramatically impacted the lives of poor Venezuelans over the past fifteen years due to the government facilitating an extensive redistribution of wealth, the delivery of free education and health care, subsidized food and housing for the poor, increased state ownership of the country's natural resources, the creation of thousands of worker-owned cooperatives and communal councils, and an astounding reduction in the number of people living in poverty from 55 percent of the population prior to Chávez's election in 1998 to 18 percent by 2011. Meanwhile, the high levels of satisfaction among Venezuelans with the country's democratic model was evident in a 2010 report issued by the region's largest polling firm, the Chile-based Corporación Latinobarómetro. According to the poll, 84 percent of Venezuelans viewed their country's democracy positively, by far the highest in the region.

The minority of Venezuelans who do not view their country as democratic are primarily from the wealthier classes. And because of their wealth, this opposition has succeeded in garnering a disproportionate amount of attention to its cause. I recall sitting with Terry in our Caracas hotel room watching the television one evening. The vehemence of the attacks on Chávez by newscasters and talk show hosts was startling. The five private television networks were owned by members of the country's wealthy elite and their programming was fiercely anti-Chávez, even going so far as to claim that the president was mentally ill and belittling him because he was part indigenous rather than white-skinned like past leaders.

Terry and I have met numerous opponents of the revolution, including a 20-year-old university student named Marcelo. We sat with Marcelo in a café in the city of Maracaibo, the country's oil capital, where he expressed his views on the revolution. He complained that the Chávez government only cared about the poor and did nothing for the wealthier sectors of Venezuelan society, including his family. Marcelo felt it was unjust that his family were now being forced to pay taxes on their second and third homes. He was referring to the fact that the government had recently passed a law exempting everyone's primary home from taxation, but second homes would be taxed at a certain rate and third homes at an even higher rate.

The government's objective was to establish housing equality in a country where a wealthy minority owned several homes while many poor were homeless or living in dilapidated shacks. It also sought to redistribute land because many of the country homes of the urban rich were massive ranches that sat idle. In the eyes of the Venezuelan government, the wealthy should either sell their excess land or pay taxes on the unproductive property so the state could use the revenues to help offset the costs of providing housing and land to the poor. The Chávez administration's land redistribution policies resulted in the transfer of ten million acres of idle land to 400,000 landless peasants.

But Marcelo and his family viewed such laws as authoritarian because they infringed on the individual property rights and privileged lifestyles of wealthy Venezuelans. According to Marcelo, the government's neglect of the wealthy meant that his family were going to have to sell one of their country homes. Evidently, he believed that his family's right to own three homes was greater than the right of a poor family to own one. In many ways, Marcelo epitomized the attitudes of Venezuela's wealthier classes who want nothing more than to return the country to the "good old days" of neoliberalism, which allowed them to freely accumulate such riches at the expense of their compatriots.

Not surprisingly, the United States has worked hard to undermine Venezuela's socialist example by implementing a variety of tactics in a long-running campaign to achieve regime change. Washington's strategy is reminiscent of its efforts that led to the 1973 ouster of the democratically-elected socialist government of President Salvador Allende in Chile. In that case, the CIA provided funding to opposition business sectors to create an economic crisis and destabilize the country to the point that a military coup could be justified. The resulting dictatorship of General Augusto Pinochet turned Chile into the initial testing ground for neoliberalism—and a human rights catastrophe.

Similarly, the United States supported the military coup in Venezuela that temporarily overthrew President Chávez in April 2002. But that plan failed when massive popular support for Chávez forced the Venezuelan military to re-instate the democratically-elected leader three days after his ouster. Following the coup debacle, Washington intensified its efforts to destabilize Venezuela by expanding its support for opposition forces under the guise of "democracy promotion." Maria Corina Machado, a leading Venezuelan opposition member involved in the coup, formed the non-governmental organization (NGO) Súmate to organize and promote a recall referendum to oust Chávez from office. The US government funded Súmate through the US Agency for International Development (USAID) and the National Endowment for Democracy (NED).

After the recall referendum also failed to remove Chávez from power in 2004, Washington further expanded its support for the opposition. A classified cable dispatched by the US Embassy in Venezuela that was published by Wikileaks reveals the USAID's objectives included penetrating Chavez' political base, dividing his support, protecting vital US business interests, and isolating Venezuela internationally. The cable goes on to note that the US strategy seeks to infiltrate President Chávez's primary support base among the poor by funding "local NGOs who work in Chavista strongholds and with Chavista leaders … with the desired effect of pulling them slowly away from Chavismo."

The USAID has spent tens of millions of dollars in Venezuela with a significant portion of the money used to fund university programs and workshops for youth, no doubt with the objective of "pulling them slowly away from Chavismo." The prominent role of university students in the 2014 protests suggests that the US strategy may be paying dividends.

As occurred in Chile, the US-backed opposition in Venezuela has created an economic crisis in recent years that is achieving its objectives of destabilizing the country and increasing disenchantment among the population. Meanwhile, the Venezuelan government hasn't helped matters due to its failure to sufficiently diversify the country's economy in order to diminish its overdependence on oil and unpredictable global energy markets. Venezuela's slow, gradual, long-term transition to socialism has also allowed the country's wealthy capitalist elites to maintain a disproportionate amount of power—particularly with regard to the economy—and they are intent on using that power to sabotage the socialist project and re-institute the neoliberal model.

Whether Venezuela's socialist revolution can survive the US-backed opposition's efforts to reverse its many achievements remains to be seen. Since World War Two, Washington has successfully ousted leftist governments throughout Latin America, including in Guatemala, Chile, Nicaragua and Haiti, that infringed on the capacity of multinational corporations to maximize profits by exploiting cheap labor and natural resources. Undoubtedly, the best known and most persistent example of US intervention has been Washington's decades-long effort to undermine Cuba's socialist example.

CHAPTER 13

An American in Havana

The launch of my book *Capitalism: A Structural Genocide* took place in April 2012 in Havana, a city I have come to love dearly. It seems fitting that the launch of my book took place in Cuba because my experiences in this country have only affirmed my belief that socialism is the most humane social system. While most tourists are charmed by the quaint 1950s cars, the beautiful colonial architecture of old Havana, and the country's pristine tropical beaches, some of the aspects of Cuba that are most visibly striking to me are the absence of advertising billboards, corporate chain stores, homeless people and violent crime.

This is not to say that Cuba is perfect, because it's not. The country still has a significant degree of centralized power in the hands of the national government and faces serious social and economic challenges resulting from the ongoing US economic blockade. But over the past two decades more power has been devolved to communities with a significant degree of participatory democracy now occurring at the municipal level. Similarly, the dismantling of large state-owned businesses and their transformation into smaller worker-managed cooperatives has increased economic democracy significantly. Consequently, as with Venezuela, I feel that Cuba provides valuable insights into the possibilities offered by socialism.

My oldest son Owen had said on numerous occasions that he would like to visit a socialist country and he finally got the opportunity when our family arrived here in June 2015. We have rented a two-bedroom apartment for three months in the Havana neighborhood of Belén. Terry is here to conduct research and I am putting the final touches on this book.

Cuba's capital is home to 2.2 million people, but the part of the city most familiar to foreign tourists is the old colonial section. This area is marked by newly-renovated buildings that host boutique hotels, restaurants, bars and shops. This neighborhood uses the tourist currency (the convertible peso, CUC) and is filled with English-speaking Cubans. But there is another side to the city that constitutes a very different world, and it is the world in which most Cubans live.

Belén is part of this world with its older buildings that are not renovated and streets that are rarely traversed by foreigners. The convertible peso, or CUC, is largely useless here because everything is purchased using the national peso. In short, Belén is a typical urban neighborhood where Cubans go about their daily activities. What quickly becomes apparent in Belén though, are the social and economic changes that have occurred in Cuba's socialist model over the past twenty years. At the root of these changes is a shift from state socialism to a more participatory model.

In the 1980s, Cuba more closely reflected the state socialist model that ultimately failed in the Soviet Union. As one Belén resident told me, "We were so dependent on the state to do everything for us that we'd call the government if we needed a light bulb changed." But with the collapse of the Soviet Union and the disintegration of the socialist trading bloc, Cuba had to become more creative if it was to survive, both literally and figuratively, as an island of socialism in an ocean of capitalism. And it was the creative survival strategies that emerged during the 1990s that have helped to redefine socialism in Cuba.

Following success in the revolutionary war in 1959, Cuba soon had to begin defending itself from US aggression. Perhaps the best known and most persistent example has been US efforts to undermine Cuba's socialist model through the ongoing economic blockade, which UN General Assembly votes have repeatedly and overwhelming condemned for the past twenty-four years including a 191-2 vote in 2015 that saw only Israel supporting Washington's targeting of the tiny island. The United States has also utilized other strategies including the Bay of Pigs invasion fiasco, many failed attempts to assassinate Fidel Castro, and CIA backing for Cuban exiles in Miami who have planted numerous bombs in Cuba and who blew up a Cuban airliner in 1976 killing all 78 people on board.

But despite being a small nation under constant attack, and with few natural resources to speak of, Cuba quickly succeeded in meeting the basic food and housing needs of all of its citizens and established free education and health care systems that are among the best in the world. However, the collapse of the Soviet Union in 1991, in conjunction with a corresponding tightening of the decades-long US blockade, meant that Cuba could no longer import sufficient food or oil. The country responded to the shortage of petroleum-based pesticides and fertilizers by becoming the world's leader in organic agriculture. It responded to the shortage of fuel by becoming a leader in urban agriculture in order to diminish the need to transport food great distances to markets. As a result, more than 85 percent of the country's agricultural production is now organic. George Lambie has called this transformation the "largest conversion from conventional agriculture to organic and semi-organic farming that the world has ever known."

This transformation is evident in communities such as Belén. We shop daily at one of the four farmers' markets situated within six blocks of our apartment that are open seven days a week. One of the markets sells produce grown on urban plots while the other three offer fruits, vegetables and meats cultivated on farms located in the green belt on the outskirts of the city.

In order to find alternatives to large-scale industrial farming and to stimulate production, the government broke-up many large state-owned farms and turned them over to the farmers as smaller worker-managed cooperatives. The new cooperatives marked a change in Cuba's socialism because they not only increased production, they also constituted a shift away from state socialism by empowering workers who previously had little or no voice in the running of their workplaces. This emerging economic democracy through cooperatives not only exists in agricultural production, it has also emerged in the selling of the goods produced. A group of community members in Belén formed the Belén Agricultural Market as a cooperative to sell the produce it purchases from a farming cooperative situated on the outskirts of the city. As a result, communities such as Belén now enjoy an abundance of inexpensive organic fruits, vegetables and meats that were harvested only hours earlier.

The shift to a more ecologically sustainable agricultural production has resulted in healthy organic food being the most convenient and inexpensive food available to Cubans. Because of the US blockade, processed foods are more expensive and not readily available. This reality stands in stark contrast to that in wealthy capitalist nations such as the United States and Canada where heavily-subsidized agri-businesses flood the market with cheap, unhealthy, processed foods while organic alternatives are expensive and more difficult to obtain. The consequences in the United States are high levels of obesity, diabetes and heart disease.

For us, in Havana, eating healthy feels like the easiest and most natural thing in the world because we are not constantly tempted by the presence—and advertising—of corporate fast food chains such as McDonalds or aisle after aisle of processed foods in the supermarkets. In fact, 90 percent of the food we consume is fresh and purchased in the neighborhood.

According to Cuban permaculturalist Roberto Pérez, Cuba established the foundation for a more ecologically sustainable society more than fifty years ago. "When the revolution gained sovereignty over the resources of the country, especially the land and the minerals, this was the base for sustainability," explained Pérez. "You cannot think about sustainability if your resources are in the hands of a foreign country or in private hands. Even without knowing, we were creating the basis for sustainability."

In 2011, the Cuban government introduced economic reforms that expanded the cooperative movement to include a variety of business sectors. While families were already permitted to open small restaurants and to rent out rooms in their homes, the latest reforms now allow people to establish small privately-owned businesses and worker-owned cooperatives in other sectors of the economy. As a result, a walk along the ten blocks of Calle Sol (Sun Street) in Belén reveals a mixture of state-owned businesses, cooperatives and small private enterprises. The bakery, two egg shops, two bars, a barber shop, a restaurant, two gyms and a convenience store are owned by the state. As previously noted, the farmers' markets are cooperatives, while private enterprises operating out of peoples' homes consist of several repair shops, an ice cream vendor, two pizza parlors, two small household goods vendors, a café, a hairdressing salon, and three coffee shops.

When the Cuban government announced in 2010 that it was going to lay off more than half a million public sector workers, the US mainstream media proclaimed the failure of socialism and a shift towards capitalism. The Cuban government's reduction in the public sector workforce was viewed in the same light as the neoliberal austerity measures implemented by capitalist nations throughout the global South. But such analysis highlighted a fundamental misunderstanding of Cuban socialism that is common in the Western mainstream media.

Unlike in capitalist nations, Cuba has not simply laid off thousands of public sector workers and left them to fend for themselves as unemployed people desperately seeking private sector jobs. The layoffs are a multi-year process and, due to the 2011 economic reforms, many workers continue to perform the same job as previously. For instance, in many service sectors, such as stores, bars, restaurants and transportation, workers have been offered the opportunity to establish cooperatives and to take over their existing places of business.

In one such case, five workers in a state-owned restaurant formed a cooperative and now lease the property from the state and run the business as their own. So while they are part of the downsizing of the public sector because they no longer work for the state, they are still performing the same job. Such a transition actually constitutes a strengthening of socialism rather than a shift towards capitalism because it is empowering workers who now have a meaningful voice in their workplace—something they didn't have under state socialism and would not have under corporate capitalism.

Further evidence that allowing small businesses and cooperatives to emerge does not necessarily represent a shift to capitalism is the fact that it remains illegal to establish a corporation. Because an individual is only permitted to own one place of business, corporate chains that monopolize production and markets cannot be established, so the overwhelming majority of businesses remain locally-owned and rooted in the community.

What Cuba is attempting to avoid are the gross inequalities that inevitably result from monopoly corporate capitalism where workers have no meaningful voice in their daily work lives and small businesses cannot compete. So while many mainstream analysts in the United States view the shift to small private businesses as a move towards capitalism, such a view ignores the fact that small privately-owned businesses are not unique to capitalism, they existed in societies long before the capitalist model came into existence.

Other aspects of Cuba's economic reality have also been seriously distorted by the US mainstream media. One such example is the reporting on salaries earned by Cubans. It is often stated that the average state salary earned by a

Cuban worker is $25 a month. While this is true, it is usually presented out of context, thereby leaving readers to believe that most Cubans must exist in dire poverty since they earn only a dollar a day. In actuality, less than 40 percent of Cubans exist solely on a state salary. The majority are earning beyond that as members of cooperatives, private entrepreneurs, state employees pocketing tips in the tourist economy, or recipients of remittances—or a combination of these.

It is true, however, that for those Cubans who do have to exist solely on a state salary life is indeed difficult. They earn just enough to cover their basic needs but can afford little else. But how can a Cuban meet his or her basic needs on only $25 a month? What most US media references to the average state salary fail to mention are the extensive state subsidies enjoyed by Cubans. All education and health care are provided free of charge as is after-school care for children. More than 80 percent of Cubans own their homes outright, therefore they pay no rent, mortgage or property tax. And electricity is heavily subsidized to the degree that most Cuban households pay about $1 a month.

Cubans also receive ration coupons that provide them with meat, eggs, bread, rice, beans, cooking oil, soap and feminine hygiene products among other essentials. The ration supplies approximately 30 percent of a person's monthly food needs, while another third is met through free lunches provided in workplaces and schools. Therefore, most Cubans only have to pay for about one-third of their monthly food needs out of pocket. Furthermore, the prices of many essentials are extremely low, allowing Cubans earning the average state salary to meet their basic needs.

For the more than 60 percent of Cubans who live on more than the average state salary, they can afford a certain amount of luxuries. This portion of the population can be seen spending convertible pesos, or CUC, in the more expensive tourist restaurants, hotels and stores as well as utilizing the public Wi-Fi hotspots that have been established throughout the island. And while the dual economies that are largely differentiated by the tourist convertible peso and the domestic national peso have resulted in greater inequality in Cuba, the country still remains the most equal in Latin America by far.

For years the US media has also suggested that Cuba's government was restricting Internet access on the island as a means of controlling the population. In reality, the inability of the country to develop the necessary infrastructure for widespread Internet usage is largely a result of the US blockade. The obvious hi-speed connection point for Cuba is to run a fiber optic cable the 90 miles from Florida to the island, but the US economic blockade has prevented this from happening. After a failed initial attempt to lay a fiber optic cable one thousand miles along the bottom of the Caribbean Sea from Venezuela to Cuba, a second attempt proved successful in 2013. This established hi-speed Internet in Havana and subsequently led to the creation of public Wi-Fi hotspots in parks and plazas throughout the country. It also led the government to slash the cost of access from $4.50 an hour to $2.00. While this still places the Internet beyond the financial means of those existing on state salaries, it has dramatically improved access for the rest of the population. This new reality is evident in the almost permanent presence in parks and plazas of people armed with their iPhones, tablets and laptops.

Cuba's socialist reforms have been implemented without any serious disruptions to the provision of free health care and education to the entire population. Cuba has one doctor for approximately every one hundred families, resulting in a ratio of physicians per 1,000 people that is the highest in the world and twice as high as in the United States. As a result, in Havana, there is a family doctor for every two blocks and each neighborhood has a polyclinic that assures access to specialists and dentists as well as providing 24-hour urgent care, with hospitals handling serious illnesses and emergencies. This is the reality in Belén, which has a 24-hour polyclinic on Sun Street and a hospital less than a mile away.

When Owen became sick one evening with a high fever, vomiting and diarrhea, we took him to the urgent care polyclinic less than a block away. He was in and out of there in fifteen minutes, having been treated by a doctor and given a shot for no charge. To our amazement, a nurse made a house call to our apartment the next day to see how Owen was doing—and he was doing fine. Our neighbors told us that the nurse's visit was not unusual; doctors and nurses regularly make house calls.

Because of the quantity of 24-hour urgent care polyclinics in addition to hospital emergency rooms, patients never have to wait long to be treated. In contrast, back home in Cape Breton, going to the emergency room at the local hospital at 9 p.m. would likely have resulted in Owen waiting for two or three hours to see a doctor. When I mentioned this to the Cuban doctor who treated Owen, she was shocked and exclaimed, "To keep a sick child waiting that long is inhumane!"

Cuba's emphasis on health care and human well-being has resulted in it achieving a life expectancy equal to the

United States and infant and child mortality rates—deaths of children under one and under five years of age respectively—that are both superior to its northern neighbor. When Cuba's health indicators are compared to capitalist nations in Latin America, the differences are astounding. Cuba's infant mortality rate of five deaths per 1,000 births compares to 19 in Mexico, 24 in Colombia and 14 in relatively wealthy Argentina. Not only are these Latin American countries capitalist nations, but they also are not forced to endure an oppressive economic blockade at the hands of the United States. In fact, many of them receive significant "development" aid from Washington and international institutions such as the World Bank.

As evidenced by its role in Venezuela, Cuba's socialist health care model is rooted in a concept of solidarity with poor and marginalized peoples throughout the world, and in Latin America and Sub-Saharan Africa in particular. Such an approach is only possible under a social system that prioritizes human well-being over profit. For example, beginning in 1997, Cuba engaged in a medical cooperation agreement with Haiti and ten years later Cuban medical staff were caring for 75 percent of that country's population. During this time, infant mortality rates per 1,000 births have plunged from 80 to 33 and life expectancy has increased from 54 years to 61 years.

Similarly, in 2004, Cuba launched "Operation Miracle" to restore eyesight to poor people throughout the global South suffering from cataracts and glaucoma. The project was initiated after Cubans engaged in literacy projects in Venezuela discovered that many poor people couldn't learn to read and write because of impaired eyesight. In its first five years, at no cost to the patients, Operation Miracle restored full eyesight to more than 1.6 million people in 28 countries and established eye surgery clinics throughout Latin America and Africa. In one case of compassionate irony, Cuban doctors working in Bolivia in 2006 restored the eyesight of the former Bolivian army sergeant who had executed Che Guevara almost forty years earlier.

Perhaps one of the most compelling examples of Cuba's international solidarity is its establishment of a medical clinic on the outskirts of Havana in 1990 to provide free health care to Ukrainian children that were sick from radiation poisoning due to the 1986 Chernobyl nuclear disaster. Over the next twenty-one years, the Tarará Clinic treated more than 25,000 Ukrainian children for cancer and other radiation-related illnesses, with some of them staying at the clinic for as long as a year at a time. The Cuban government covered all the costs of room, board, medical treatment and schooling for each of the children, with medical costs alone estimated to have totaled more than $300 million. The Cuban economy received no benefits from treating those children; in fact, the Tarará Clinic constituted a drain on the country's economy. Nevertheless, Cuba's socialist system treated those children who could not afford medical care back home because human well-being is prioritized over economic growth.

Ultimately, Cuba seeks to train domestic personnel in the countries in which it works so they can eventually operate their own health care systems. To this end, the Cuban government provides scholarships annually to thousands of people from nations throughout the global South to attend a Cuban medical school. The only condition placed on the scholarships is that the new doctors return home to practice medicine among the poor for a minimum of five years rather than emigrating with their newfound skills to wealthy capitalist nations as part of the brain drain from the global South to the global North. Tellingly, Cuba's number one export is health care. This contrasts dramatically with the leading export of the United States, which is weaponry.

In 2013, I met a family in Cuba's second-largest city, Santiago de Cuba, that encapsulates the country's emerging economic democracy and its international solidarity. Rolando was 42-years-old and a member of a five-person cooperative that operated a small restaurant in the city center. The cooperative leased the formerly state-run business from the government and its members now make all decisions collectively and distribute earnings according to the number of hours each of them work. Meanwhile, Rolando's wife Yamile is a doctor who had recently returned from working with a Cuban medical mission in Venezuela's poor barrios.

As Rolando and Yamile illustrate, the result of Cuba's socialist model is a highly educated and healthy population. Furthermore, homelessness, malnutrition and violent crime—social maladies that are rampant in capitalist Latin American nations—are conspicuous by their absence in Cuban society. Cuba's lack of violent crime is particularly noteworthy given that 18 of the top 20 cities with the highest homicide rates in the world are located in Latin America. And the lack of violent crime in Cuba is not due to an excessive police presence. In fact, I have never seen so few police officers or private armed security guards in a large Latin American city as in Havana. I would argue that public safety in Cuba is a result of the population internalizing socialist values over the past half-century that are rooted in compassion, cooperation and solidarity.

The sense of safety in Havana is palpable. Owen and Morgan regularly play after dark in the plazas with nine and ten year-old Cuban children whose parents are nowhere to be seen. It is common for children to go out alone to public places several blocks from their home to play with their peers. And Terry feels a degree of safety when walking the streets of Havana alone, even at two o'clock in the morning, that she has never before experienced in a large city.

Based on the country's environmental practices and its social indicators, the World Wildlife Fund's "Living Planet Report" declared that Cuba is the only nation in the world to have achieved sustainable development. In other words, Cuba is the only country that is successfully meeting the basic needs of its entire population in an ecologically sustainable manner. Meanwhile, the same WWF report noted that more than four Planet Earths would be required for everyone in the world to live in the same manner as people in the United States. Furthermore, Cuba's scientific achievements in the field of medicine and its successes with sustainable organic agriculture dispel the myth that innovation is unique to capitalism.

Despite all of the benefits that Cubans enjoy from the country's socialist system, some people naturally still harbor frustrations. The most common complaints are low salaries and over-crowded housing. The country's youth also yearn for greater access to the Internet. Consequently, some Cubans see a shift towards capitalism as a possible solution to these problems and for achieving a more luxurious lifestyle. Cubans are inundated with capitalist propaganda in the form of Hollywood movies and TV shows as well as the Internet. Younger generations in particular—those too young to recall life prior to 1959 who take the revolution's social achievements for granted—are being seduced by the capitalist consumer dream; and this, perhaps more than anything else, poses the greatest threat to Cuba's socialist model.

This seduction is not surprising given that it is the luxurious lifestyles of the upper-middle and upper classes in the United States that dominate movies and TV as well as the Internet. And, in conjunction with the seemingly endless flow of relatively rich foreign tourists that visit Cuba from wealthy capitalist nations, some Cubans associate capitalism with material wealth. But only 20 percent of the world's population live in the manner of people in the capitalist nations of North America and Europe. The majority of those living under capitalism in the global South endure poverty and misery. This inequality is inevitable under capitalism because the Earth cannot sustain seven billion people living in the manner that North Americans live. Therefore, the wealthy nations are required to consume a disproportionate percentage of the planet's resources to maintain their standards of living, and they do so by taking the resources of the poor.

Geographically, the closest capitalist country to Cuba is not the United States, it is Haiti, where 70 percent of the population lives in poverty and life expectancy is 20 years less than in Cuba. The poverty endured by Haitians is far more reflective of the reality of most people in the world who live under capitalism than the standard of living of North Americans. But the plight of Haitians is rarely seen in Hollywood movies and on TV shows. It is rarely front and center on the Internet. It remains the hidden face of global capitalism.

Given that Haiti is a capitalist nation, it is clear that capitalism in and of itself does not guarantee a luxurious standard of living for all people, or even a majority—or Haitians would live like most North Americans. It is the combination of capitalism and imperialism that has created wealth in rich nations and poverty in poor nations—and, ultimately, structural genocide. The United States, Canada and Western European countries are imperialist powers because they wield a hugely disproportionate amount of influence over neo-colonial institutions such as the United Nations, the IMF and the World Bank in addition to the coercive capacities of their own foreign policies.

But Cuba is not an imperialist nation. Therefore, a dismantling of socialism and a shift to capitalism would not allow Cubans to live as most North Americans do. Capitalism in Cuba would more closely reflect the reality of Haiti, Honduras, Guatemala, Colombia and many other Latin American nations struggling with poverty, inequality and violence. Capitalism would generate wealth for perhaps 20 percent of the population while half of Cubans would likely endure poverty. In fact, not only would half the population still not have access to luxuries under capitalism, but they would also likely lose the social benefits they currently enjoy under socialism in the form of health care, education, food, housing and crime-free neighborhoods.

The lack of awareness among North Americans regarding Cuba's impressive social and environmental achievements is quite stunning. It further highlights the power of capitalist propaganda. Many Canadians I talk to who have visited Cuba on vacation comment on the poverty in the country. This is not surprising given that they are comparing the material wealth—and environmentally unsustainable lifestyle—that exists in an imperialist capitalist nation like Canada with a non-imperialist socialist country. Many Canadians respond to the relative poverty in Cuba by concluding that socialism doesn't work. Interestingly, those who return from vacation trips to the Dominican Republic,

Mexico or other capitalist nations in Latin America don't respond to the poverty that exists in those countries by declaring that capitalism doesn't work.

It seems to me that most people in wealthy nations equate capitalism with a high materialistic standard of living and therefore don't consider poor countries in Latin America, Africa and Asia to be capitalist. But this is a selective and flawed defining of capitalism. In actuality, the overwhelming majority of nations in the global South have been capitalist nations for hundreds of years and have played—and continue to play—a crucial role in a global capitalist system that has generated great wealth for the global North while condemning half of the world's population to a life of poverty and more than ten million annually to death. And yet "poverty" in Cuba is blamed on socialism while poverty in Haiti, the Dominican Republic, Mexico, Angola, Nigeria, Bangladesh and other poor countries in the global South is somehow not the fault of capitalism but of corruption or ineptitude or some other inexplicable and mysterious set of circumstances.

Each time I travel to Cuba I feel uplifted and inspired by the degree to which the country's socialist experiment continues to try to create a society marked by human and social development rather than the consumerism and materialism emphasized in a capitalist system dominated by the culture of individualism. As Fidel Castro claimed in 2005, Cuba "will never be a society of consumption … It will be a society of knowledge, of culture, of the most extraordinary human development that one can imagine." While Cuba has not yet fully achieved such an exalted state, its socialist model has addressed the plight of the poor in Cuba and throughout much of the global South far more effectively than has capitalism.

Most Cubans recognize the Revolution's social achievements and, as a result, would like to preserve the socialist model, albeit with a few more material comforts. But as long as the world remains dominated by capitalism there will be limits to the degree of material comfort that Cubans can obtain. On the other hand, if a significant socialist bloc were to emerge then a more equitable distribution of the planet's resources might indeed be possible, which would not only improve the standard of living of many Cubans but also of those impoverished billions throughout the global South existing—and dying—under capitalism's structural genocide.

Having witnessed the socialist models being implemented in Venezuela and Cuba I believe it is possible to achieve a more democratic and sustainable global society that prioritizes the well-being of all people. Through worker-owned cooperatives and participatory democracy at the grassroots level we can become empowered and gain a meaningful voice in all of the major decisions that impact our lives. For me, a society marked by grassroots participatory democracy, sustainable development, collective well-being, individual enlightenment, vibrant communities and a healthy planet constitutes socialism. And this is why I'm a socialist.

CONCLUSION

A Few Final Thoughts …

My journey to socialism has been a long one and will most likely entail many more twists and turns in the future. While I have long questioned the legitimacy of capitalism as a result of my personal experiences, it took a number of years before I began seriously exploring viable alternatives. Consequently, I didn't begin self-defining as a socialist until I was in my early forties. More specifically, as the title of this book states, I identify as an "American" socialist. Not only am I a US citizen who has lived the majority of his life in North America, but I have also worked extensively in Latin America where many people consider anyone from any part of the Americas to be an "American." And it is more in keeping with this latter, broader definition of American that I identify as an American socialist.

On the surface, my life might appear to have been little more than a series of disconnected adventures and experiences in a variety of locales. But in actuality it has been a journey whose path has been determined, often subconsciously, by a desire to be true to myself. And because I was so wrapped up in my selfishness during many of those early years, I remained in denial of the very essence of my being: my humanity.

Undoubtedly I'm still individualistic, but I now like to think of myself as an individual with a social conscience. Instead of feeling isolated and alienated, and responding to that condition by exhibiting selfishness and self-indulgence, I now try to use the skill-set that I've acquired through my life experiences to become a more compassionate person working for the greater social good. This growing sense of myself, and awareness of the kind of world that I not only want to live in, but in which I would like my children and grandchildren to live, provides me with a true sense of purpose.

Terry has been crucial in this process. Her unwavering compassion and commitment to discovering the truth is a constant inspiration. She keeps me honest by simply being who she is. Over the years Terry has become increasingly involved in Buddhism. Her melding of her personal Buddhist philosophy with her broader socialist beliefs has only pushed me to try to better reflect the famous Gandhi quote, "Be the change that you want to see in the world." It's easy to criticize the shortcomings of others and the society in which we live, but Terry has made me fully realize how much more challenging it is to honestly reflect on our own flaws. She has had a similar influence on Owen and Morgan, thereby softening some of the harder edges they get from me and helping them to develop into compassionate human beings.

Many of my experiences, particularly my work in Colombia, have resulted in me developing a great deal of compassion for those who have suffered gross injustices. While this in and of itself is not necessarily revolutionary, I think that the desire to change things in order to bring an end to such injustices is. The ability to feel the pain and suffering of others, even those we don't know or don't like, and to try to understand them makes it easier for one to respond with tolerance and compassion. It also allows one to be strong enough to forgive. It is easy to exhibit compassion for victims. In fact, a failure to do so is cruel. But the real challenge is showing compassion to the abuser. And yet, such compassion is essential if we are to live in a world free from violence. Ultimately, such compassion allows all of us to express our humanity.

I believe that capitalism is incompatible with such a vision, and that only socialism can produce a compassionate society capable of valuing compassionate individuals. In contrast, capitalism often sees compassion and caring for others as weaknesses; instead viewing self-interest, aggression and competitiveness as desirable traits. It is up to all of us to make a compassionate society a global reality. After all, the capitalists who own and manage the multinational corporations are not the only ones responsible for the structural genocide that is occurring globally. We all need to take a closer look in the mirror because too many of our lifestyle choices make us complicit in the structural genocide that kills more than ten million people annually. Given this reality, it's crucial that we work together collectively to implement a radical alternative to capitalism in order to achieve a more compassionate, humane and sustainable global society.

Many claim that radical alternatives are "unrealistic," but it has become glaringly obvious to me that it's the belief we can continue with the existing model that is unrealistic. Therefore, we need to heed the words of Vandana Shiva and "take less" from the global South, because the only reason we've been able to maintain our relatively luxurious lifestyles in the global North is by consuming other peoples' share of the planet's resources and by exploiting their labor. But sadly there is little desire in the global North to address the injustices that result from capitalism in order to end the ecological destruction and the structural genocide because, as environmental activist George Monbiot has pointed out, "We are simply too comfortable and we have too much to lose." In truth, we all have much more to lose if we don't act.

Therefore, the only response to the unsustainable model of global capitalism is for us to wage a revolution within ourselves. First, we must revolutionize the way we think. And then, we must revolutionize the way we live. The principal obstacle to convincing people in the global North to become engaged in such a revolution is the strongly held belief that their happiness is directly linked to their materially comfortable lifestyle. In other words, if people in the global North were to experience a reduction in their level of material comfort, then they would not be as happy. But recent studies have suggested that there is no correlation between income and happiness once earnings surpass the amount required to subsist. As Richard Layard, director of the Well-Being Programme at the London School of Economics has noted, "Over the last 50 years, living standards in the West have improved enormously but we have become no happier. This shows we should not sacrifice human relationships, which are the main source of happiness, for the sake of economic growth." And yet, in the individualistic consumer culture that dominates capitalism, sacrificing human relationships—rupturing and dislocating families and communities—is exactly what we've done in our quest for greater levels of material comfort.

So if people living in wealthy capitalist societies are no happier today than they were half a century ago despite dramatic increases in income, why do we continually strive to earn more money in order to purchase more things? Part of the problem is linked to the concept of "relative deprivation," which argues that it is not only poverty that breeds discontent, but also the perception that our social status is lower than that of our neighbors or others in our society. Karl Marx illustrated this concept when he wrote, "A house may be large or small; as long as the surrounding houses are equally small, it satisfies all social demands for a dwelling. But if a palace rises beside the little house, the little house shrinks into a hut." In our capitalist consumer culture, our sense of self-worth is measured by the material possessions we own: the size of our house, the model of car we drive, the clothes we wear, and so on. Ultimately then, the perpetual quest to achieve ever-higher levels of material comfort under global capitalism is not only environmentally unsustainable, it is also spiritually unfulfilling because it fails to increase our happiness.

Furthermore, the belief that we can achieve sustainable development in wealthy nations such as the United States and Canada without dramatically diminishing our levels of material comfort is a form of denial that allows us to believe that we can have our cake and eat it too. Such denial is not surprising. After all, the idea of dramatically reducing our material consumption is anathema both to corporations and to consumers who have been indoctrinated to associate success and happiness with material wealth.

Capitalism requires a constantly expanding production and consumption of goods, which can only be achieved through the increased exploitation of the planet's natural resources at an unsustainable rate. Because of this reality, sustainable development cannot be achieved without a dramatic reduction in the levels of production and consumption, which directly contradicts the growth logic that drives capitalism. But while achieving such extensive reductions would indeed be challenging, they are possible.

The United Nations has noted that when the UN Human Development Index is combined with the per capita ecological footprint of 182 nations as determined by the Global Footprint Network, only one country has a genuinely sustainable economy. That country is Cuba. In other words, Cuba is the only country in the world that has met the basic needs—food, housing, health and education—of all of its citizens in an ecologically sustainable manner. It is no coincidence that the only country to achieve sustainable development is a socialist nation.

All other nations have achieved either one (high human development) or the other (small ecological footprint) of the two objectives, but not both. Wealthy nations score very high in the human development index but have per capita ecological footprints far beyond the sustainable 1.7 global hectares. For example, the United States and Canada both rank "very high" in human development but their per capita ecological footprints are 6.8 and 6.6 global hectares respectively. Consequently, we would need four planet Earths for everyone in the world to live the lifestyle enjoyed by North Americans.

Conversely, most poor nations have a sustainable per capita ecological footprint below 1.7 global hectares but rank in the "low" category of human development. Angola, for example, has a very sustainable per capita ecological footprint of 0.9 global hectares but ranks "low" in the human development index at 149th in the world. This is because almost half of Angolans live in poverty and consume few resources while enduring a life expectancy of only 51 years and receiving a mere 4.7 years of education.

The realities of wealthy nations (high human development and large ecological footprint) and poor nations (low human development and small ecological footprint) are directly linked. Because we only have one planet Earth, the unsustainably large ecological footprints of wealthy nations such as the United States and Canada are achieved by North Americans consuming other peoples' share of the planet's resources. As a result, the resources of poor countries are exploited not for the benefit of local populations but to satiate the consumption appetites of wealthy nations.

Because we in the wealthy nations of the global North can only sustain our materialistically comfortable lifestyles by consuming other peoples' share of the planet's resources, we condemn those people to a shortened life of poverty and misery. As a result, more than ten million people die needlessly each year from hunger as well as from preventable and treatable diseases under the global capitalist system. The gross inequalities inherent in capitalism are also a major cause of wars, terrorism, mass migration, refugees, human trafficking and escalating criminal violence throughout much of the global South. Our unsustainable lifestyle is not only causing massive human suffering and death for millions around the world today, it is destroying the planet for future generations.

There is no silver bullet that will allow us to painlessly achieve sustainable development. Many believe—or hope—technology will provide a miraculous solution that will allow us to consume sustainably in the future at current levels. But despite all of the impressive technological advances of the past half-century, the extent of ecological damage to the planet has not decreased but increased during this period. Ultimately then, if we are serious about achieving a more sustainable and just development, we must dramatically diminish our levels of material consumption, which contravenes the very logic that drives the capitalist system.

But how do we make implementing an extreme shift in our consumption-driven lifestyles appealing to the majority of North Americans and Europeans? We need to change our mindset regarding the sources of success and happiness. Instead of measuring success and happiness by income earned and material possessions consumed, we need to focus on quality of life.

A massive reduction in our consumption habits would mean that we could work far fewer hours in order to support ourselves. Currently, half the world's population works too many hours while the other half is effectively unemployed and engaged in a desperate struggle for survival. An equal distribution of the planet's resources and workload would allow all workers to be productive members of society while also enjoying ample leisure time. The corresponding increase in leisure time would allow us to engage in self-education to learn more about ourselves and the world in which we live. It would also allow us to focus more time and energy developing and sustaining meaningful relationships in our families and our communities, and for engaging in creative activities. Finally, reducing our levels of consumption would ensure that there are sufficient natural resources left on the planet to sustain our children and grandchildren.

At its core, the history of capitalism is the history of the struggle between the haves and the have-nots. Under neoliberal globalization, economic elites in both the North and South have increased their share of the wealth at the expense of the majority. And while the quality of life for most in the global North has deteriorated under globalization, much of the population still enjoys a relatively high level of material comfort when compared to the majority of people in the global South. In other words, under globalization, a significant portion of the population of the global North constitute, to varying degrees, the haves, while the majority in the South represent the have-nots—with little hope of improving their lot.

So while, for the most part, I feel largely at peace with myself at this point in my life, this peace comes with a certain level of discomfort because I do not exist in a void—I am an individual who lives in a global social context. It is difficult to look at the suffering and misery that is so prevalent in the world and feel optimistic; but not caring is not an option. This does not mean that I don't become discouraged and cynical at times. There are periods when I become incredibly frustrated at the deep entrenchment of capitalist values in our society and the lack of caring and apathy that results. But somehow the belief that the choices I make in my life can, in some small way, make the world a better place for at least a few people always seems to prevail. Regardless of whether or not we feel we can effect change for the better during our time here on Earth, there's a personal satisfaction in doing the right thing, the moral thing. This pessimist-optimist contradiction that I regularly experience was best summed up by Italian socialist Antonio Gramsci when he stated, "I'm a pessimist because of intelligence, but an optimist because of will."

Gandhi said that a person who seeks the truth will inevitably be drawn into politics. And, given my experiences in Britain, the United States, Canada and Latin America, I have come to the same conclusion. We are all political beings; our only choices rest in whether or not we choose to acknowledge this fact and how we decide to act on it. It has become clear to me that the maintenance of our comfortable consumer and materialistic lifestyles in North America and Europe is inextricably linked to environmental devastation and the structural genocide that kills millions of people annually in the global South. An acknowledgement of this reality, and a desire to act on it, combined with the capacity to exhibit compassion and love for our fellow beings, can only result in the creation of a revolutionary individual. And if we are to combat such global injustices, then revolutionary individuals will need to work together collectively.

Both Owen and Morgan are homeschooled and part of their curriculum involves discussing many of the issues I have addressed in this book. Terry and I try to ensure that Owen and Morgan are aware of the global inequalities that exist and how their unearned privilege as white middle-class males means they inevitably benefit from those inequalities. We don't do this to induce guilt in them, but in the hope that they'll become compassionate people who develop a desire to challenge any system that causes such injustices and human suffering. Similarly, I try to create the same awareness among my students and my readers about how these global injustices are intimately connected to their lives.

There are, however, limits to what we can achieve through transforming ourselves and the way we live as individuals. The capitalist system of production and distribution pervades virtually every area of our daily lives and it has become difficult to find alternative ways to obtain many of our necessities. Whether we are buying groceries for our families, or shoes and clothes for our children, we are intimately linked to the global process of exploitation. Therefore, in order to confront some of the broader structures of capitalism, we need to work together collectively to challenge the existing system at the local, national and international levels if we are to have any hope of establishing a more democratic, humane and sustainable global alternative.

One of the barriers to bringing about such far-reaching change is the superficial concept of individualism that has become so dominant under capitalism, and which has caused us to lose the ability to fulfill the social aspect of our being in any meaningful way. The result is a society of individuals without a collective conscience, which compels us to consume more and more material goods in a desperate attempt to escape our alienated state. Therefore, it is essential that we begin to correct this imbalance between our individualistic side and our social side and re-establish some sort of equilibrium. This process will require a lot of self-introspection on the individual level and revolutionary organization on the collective level.

I believe that such a personal and collective transformation would inevitably lead to the establishment of a socialist society. Not an authoritarian socialist society in which dogmatic ideas are imposed on us by the state, but a democratic socialism that is participatory in nature because it gives all of us a meaningful voice in all of the major decisions that impact our lives. Consequently, achieving a socialist society requires that each of us at the individual level exhibit compassion and a sense of fairness towards all. In essence, we would still focus on our own self-interest, but we would recognize that our own interests are intimately linked to those of everyone else on the planet and to the planet itself.

While there are some fundamental principles upon which to base a socialist society, there is no one-size-fits-all blueprint. Consequently, the precise form that socialism takes will vary from community to community and society to society. In some collective cultures it might not be called socialism, even though the fundamental values of the society reflect socialist ideals—which is the case with many indigenous cultures.

There is no guarantee that socialism will emerge after capitalism self-destructs under its greed-driven logic. There is always the possibility that we will devolve into some sort of violent barbaric state due to the desperation of the billions of people sacrificed under capitalism and the environmental harm done to the planet. But the future no longer simply consists of "socialism or barbarism," as Rosa Luxemburg famously suggested a century ago. We are now facing a third possibility: the annihilation of the human race and the extermination of life on Planet Earth, which would constitute the ultimate genocidal act perpetrated by capitalism. Therefore, our choice now consists of socialism, barbarism or extermination. And it's up to us to make this choice.

In actuality, we have no choice. We have to wage a revolution to establish a more democratic, humane and sustainable world if humanity is to survive. Some might think that I and others like me are unrealistic, that we are dreamers. But I would like to respond to such assertions with the immortal words of Che: "And if it were said of us that we're almost romantics, that we are incorrigible idealists, that we think the impossible: then a thousand and one times we have to answer that yes, we are."

The number of romantic idealists in the wealthy nations of the global North appears to be on the rise in recent years. This reality is evident in the emergence of the Occupy and Idle No More movements in North America and the mass protests of recent years against IMF-imposed austerity measures in Spain and Greece. The fact polls show that more US youth prefer socialism to capitalism is further evidence, as is the public response to the US presidential candidacy of self-proclaimed socialist Bernie Sanders. And in Britain it is evidenced by that country's Labour Party recently electing socialist Jeremy Corbyn as its leader.

It is on the heels of this growing socialist movement in the global North that Owen and Morgan are growing up. Therefore, I am hopeful that they'll grow up into a more democratic, humane and sustainable world—a socialist world. A world that not only benefits them and others in the global North, but also my daughter Johan and grandchildren Kathleen and Dylan, as well as everyone else in the global South.

In closing, I would like to recall a sunny afternoon in May 2014 when I passed by the Tarará Clinic on the outskirts of Havana. I couldn't help but think of the political turmoil that was occurring in Ukraine at that moment. I also couldn't help but reflect on the stark contrast between Cuba's humanitarian relationship with that troubled country and the self-serving Machiavellian machinations of the world's leading capitalist powers—the United States, EU, Russia and Canada. For more than twenty years, Cuba's selfless provision of free health care, shelter, food and education to Ukrainian children afflicted with cancer and other sicknesses caused by radiation poisoning was rooted in a compassionate solidarity that prioritized the needs of human beings over economic

CONCLUSION

growth. It reflected all that is noble about the human spirit. It also reflected the core values of socialism.

It is in accordance with those values that I intend to continue my daily struggle to achieve a more just and compassionate society on a global scale, inspired by the increasing numbers of people throughout the world who are also looking for a more sustainable and humane alternative to the genocidal capitalist system. After all, it's the least I can do for my children and grandchildren.

ABOUT THE AUTHOR

Garry Leech is an independent journalist and author of seven other books including *Capitalism: A Structural Genocide* (Zed Books, 2012); *Beyond Bogotá: Diary of a Drug War Journalist in Colombia* (Beacon Press, 2009); and *Crude Interventions: The United States, Oil and the New World Disorder* (Zed Books, 2006). He also teaches international politics at Cape Breton University in Nova Scotia, Canada and Javeriana University in Cali, Colombia.

INDEX

Allende, Salvador, 73, 155
al-Qaeda, 106, 110
Amazon Rainforest, 51-60, 90, 99, 110, 130
Amnesty International, 115
Angola, 174, 181
Arauca (Colombia), 111-112, 115-117
Argentina, 90, 168
Atlacatl Battalion (El Salvador), 43
Atlantic Ocean, 8, 52
Atlantic Regional Solidarity Network (ARSN), 128
AUC (Auto-Defensas Unidas de Colombia), 97, 102
austerity, 3, 76, 78, 80, 163, 188
Australia, 7

Bangladesh, 174
Bay of Pigs, 160
Belén (Cuba), 159, 161, 163, 167
Berlin Wall, 52, 148-149
Boesky, Ivan, 72
Bogotá (Colombia), 113-114
Bramhall, 5, 11
Buddhism, 177
Bush, George H.W., 51, 72
Bush, George W., 109-110, 114, 116-117

Canada, 7, 45-46, 68-69, 73, 79-80, 122-123, 126-127, 162, 173, 180-182, 185, 188
Cape Breton (Canada), 126-127, 143, 167
Caracas, 148, 150, 153
Carter, Jimmy, 1
Castaño, Carlos, 97
Castro, Fidel, 90, 160, 174
Cerrejón Mine (Colombia), 128-129
Chávez, Hugo, 148-149, 151-156
Chernobyl, 169
Chile, 73-75, 79, 90, 153, 155-157
China, 81
Chippendale, William, 4
Chiquita Brands, 97
Chomsky, Noam, 68
Clinton, Bill, 73, 94
Coca-Cola, 56-58
cocaine, 27, 51, 95-96, 111
Cold War, 2, 52, 75
Colombia, 22, 51-52, 90, 94-99, 104-106, 110-122, 124, 127-130, 132-135, 143-144, 148, 168, 173
Conservative, Party (Britain), 73

INDEX

Conservative Party (Canada), 73
Corbyn, Jeremy, 3, 188
Costa Rica, 30, 51
Coventry, 4-5, 7, 14
Cruz, Francisco Javier, 111-112
Cuba, 1, 148, 152, 157-175, 181, 188-189

Democratic Party, 12, 73
Dervis, Kermal, 139
Detroit, 8-10, 14, 26, 30, 42, 49-51, 65, 82, 87, 127
displacement, 80-81, 115, 118, 128-130, 132, 134-135
Dominican Republic, 6, 65, 173-174

Ecuador, 51, 52, 101, 110, 130
Einstein, Albert, 85, 87
El Mozote Massacre (El Salvador), 44, 77
El Salvador, 31-41, 43-45, 75, 77-79, 95, 100, 109-110, 123, 134
England, 4, 11, 13, 45, 88, 123
European Union (EU), 188

FARC (Fuerzas Armadas Revolucionarias de Colombia), 96, 98, 110
Farmer, Paul, 136
Friedman, Milton, 68-69, 74-75

Gandhi, Mohandas, 88-93, 177, 185
genocide, 131, 142, 158, 173, 175, 178-179, 185
Gibbs, Terry, 122-126, 143-144, 148-150, 153, 159, 171, 177, 185
Global Footprint Network, 181
Gramsci, Antonio, 185
Great Britain, 2-3, 6-7, 9, 69, 73, 123, 185, 188
Great Depression, 4, 7, 68
Greece, 3, 188
Greenspan, Alan, 70
Guajira (Colombia), 130, 132-133
Guantanamo Bay, 2
Guatemala, 40, 157, 173
Guevara, Ernesto "Che", 90-93, 169, 188

Halifax (Canada), 129
Haiti, 157, 168, 172-174
Havana, 1, 158-159, 162, 166-167, 169-171, 188
health care (Canada), 127, 167
health care (Cuba), 160, 165, 167-170, 173, 189
health care (US), 65-67, 168
health care (Venezuela), 151-153
Hoagland, Eros, 99-104
Honduras, 30-31, 173

Howe, Jason, 112-114, 124

Idle No More Movement, 3, 188
India, 131
Indignados, 3, 188
inequality, 2, 71, 77-78, 118, 127, 131, 133, 134, 136-137, 139, 141, 166, 172-173
International Monetary Fund (IMF), 75-76, 78, 80, 96, 134, 141, 173, 188
International Red Cross, 39-40
Iraq, 114, 117

Keynesian, 4, 68, 75, 77
Kissinger, Henry, 73

Labour Party (Britain), 3, 7, 188
Las Vegas, 61, 64-65, 83-85, 88
Layard, Richard, 179
London School of Economics, 179
Los Angeles, (Colombia), 100
Los Angeles (US), 16-17, 111

Manchester, 5, 8
Marx, Karl, 133, 146, 180
Massey Ferguson, 5, 8, 45-47, 98
Mexico, 64, 79-82, 109, 168, 174

Michigan, 9, 16, 25, 27, 30
Milken, Michael, 72
Miller, Judith, 114
Monbiot, George, 179
Mulroney, Brian, 69

Napo River (Ecuador), 52-56, 59
National Endowment for Democracy (NED), 155
Neoliberalism, 69, 71-80, 82, 95-96, 117-120, 127-128, 130-131, 134, 137, 145-146, 148, 150-151, 154-156, 163, 184
New York City, 49-50, 61, 64-65, 70-72, 84, 94, 104, 121-122, 124, 126
New Zealand, 7
Nicaragua, 30, 34, 51, 79, 123, 157
Nigeria, 174
Nixon, Richard, 12
Noriega, Manuel, 51, 145
North American Congress on Latin America (NACLA), 94-95, 122-123, 126
North American Free Trade Agreement (NAFTA), 79-82, 134
Northville, 8-9, 11, 13, 26-27
Nova Scotia Power (NSP), 127, 129-130

INDEX

Occidental Petroleum, 111, 116
Occupy Movement, 3, 188

Panama, 21-25, 30, 51-52, 144-146
Panama City, 22-23, 30, 51, 145
paramilitaries, 97, 100, 115-116
Pérez, José Julio, 129-130
Pérez, Lisandro, 148
Pérez, Roberto, 162
Pinochet, Augusto, 73-74, 155
Plan Colombia, 94, 96, 98-99, 110-112
Porto Alegre, 122, 124
poverty, 23, 63, 77-78, 98, 120-121, 123, 130-131, 133-134, 139, 145, 148, 153, 165, 172-174, 181-182
Putumayo (Colombia), 99, 111

Ramírez, Francisco, 120
Rand, Ayn, 25, 27-30, 42, 44-45, 47, 61-63, 66, 69-70, 88
Reagan, Ronald, 2, 29, 51, 67-73, 76-77
Reaganomics, 68, 71, 73
Republican Party, 12, 73
Richardson, Bill, 96
Romero, Oscar, 43, 77
Ruiz, Louisa, 150

Russia, 188

Sanders, Bernie, 3, 188
Santana, Luis Alberto, 116
Saravena (Colombia), 112, 114-116, 125
Shiva, Vandana, 130-134, 178
Smith, Patti, 31, 40
Soviet Union, 1-2, 28, 147, 159-160
Spain, 3, 188
Stiglitz, Joseph, 69, 76
Stone, Oliver, 43
Súmate (Venezuela), 155
Sydney (Canada), 126

Tabaco (Colombia), 128-130
Tarará Clinic (Cuba), 169, 188
Thatcher, Margaret, 62, 69

Ukraine, 188
UN Development Program (UNDP), 136, 139
UN Human Development Index, 181
UNICEF, 136
unions, 7, 49, 66-67, 70, 97, 112, 115-116, 120, 126-127
United Nations, 135, 173, 181
United States, 1-3, 7-8, 10, 12-13, 15, 17, 22, 25, 28, 34-35, 42-43, 45-46, 58-59, 65, 67-70, 73, 75-82, 85,

87, 96, 109-110, 114, 126, 127, 134, 136, 138, 155, 160, 162, 164, 167-168, 170-173, 180-182, 185-188
University of Chicago, 68, 74
University of Nevada, Las Vegas (UNLV), 65, 68, 83, 94
Uribe, Alvaro, 115, 117
US Agency for International Development (AID), 155-156
US Army, 17, 21, 23-24, 111-112, 114, 116
US Congress, 109-110
US Marines, 16-17, 20-21, 24-26, 34, 41, 60, 145
US Military, 17, 21-22, 43, 52, 77-78, 94-95, 111, 115-118, 120, 145
US Navy, 21
US State Department, 97, 118

Venezuela, 148-157, 159, 166, 168, 170, 175

Vietnam War, 12, 77

Wall Street, 71-72, 82
war on terror, 22, 97, 106, 109-119
Washington, DC, 22, 52, 68, 73, 76, 83-84, 110, 119, 155-157, 160, 168
Watergate, 12
Wayúu (Colombia), 129-130, 132-133
Wikileaks, 156
Woods, James, 43
World Bank, 69, 75-76, 134, 141, 168, 173
World Health Organization, 136
World Social Forum, 122-123
World Trade Center, 105, 108
World Trade Organization (WTO), 134, 141
World War Two, 4, 7, 52, 157
World Wildlife Fund (WWF), 171
Wright, Thomas, 68

www.ingramcontent.com/pod-product-compliance
Lightning Source LLC
Chambersburg PA
CBHW050536300426
44113CB00012B/2120